'MARATHON MADGE'

by

Madge Sharples

To June and Glyn
Happiest of Aberdare memories!
Love and Best Wishes

MRG Publications, Hyde, Cheshire. 1989

Madge

First published in Great Britain by
MRG Publications
Onward Chambers, 34 Market Street
Hyde, Cheshire SK14 1AH

ISBN 0 9514575 0 0

Printed and Bound in Great Britain by
Pindar Group, Scarborough

Set in Times New Roman

To Fred, Edward, Adam and Barbara,
Vivien and Stephen, Ella and Reg.

Acknowledgements

I wish to thank Mel the Editor, Colin the Sub-Editor, and Steve for their devoted and meticulous care in the production of this book.

Preface

Marathon running is the ripe fruit of a slow-growing tree, a tree that has its roots in our habits, our life-styles and our individual determination. The seed from which the tree has grown, our forebears, plays a big part too. But, whatever the seed, and whatever the shape our fitness tree has grown into, we can prune it and encourage new growth to develop. We can start to improve our fitness and our ability to run, right away. And in this book, I hope I'm going to help you to do just that. I know we can't all be runners – those that can, do, and those that can't, teach – but we can all be fitter, tackle jobs with more gusto and speed, and get more enjoyment out of life.

It's up to you to improve your own health and well-being. The longest journey starts with but one step. Let that step be a mental one. Sit back and see the fitter, healthier more attractive you. Imagine the exciting things you'll be able to achieve. Oscar Wilde wrote, "Fashion is so intolerable, it has to be changed every six months." Think of your body changing over the months, *for the better*.

Running has certainly changed mine. I'm slimmer, straighter (when I remember) and more energetic. And my daughter Vivien no longer greets me when she comes home after an absence with, "How's your alkie problem, Mummy?" So, perhaps reading of how I got started might help you. I hope it does.

Contents

Madge today

1 Background

"Doctor, am I going to kill myself in this marathon?" It was just before the first Gillette London Marathon, that was run on 29 March 1981, when, aged 64, I was the oldest woman competitor. "That's something no medico can tell", he answered, "anything can happen in a marathon." And 'anything' did happen, and hasn't stopped yet.

I found myself catapulted into a new world, of television and radio, athletes and runners, journalists and joggers, and everywhere, friendly, smiling faces. What made it all happen was the luck of being ready, in the right place at the right time, to take part in Chris Brasher's inspired idea.

Running a marathon was light years away from my life-style as a home-and-garden-loving mother of Edward, Adam, Vivien and Steve, working with the Royal Army Pay Corps at Worthy Down, Winchester. But I managed it, and now, forty-seven completed marathons later, I'm planning my next, and the next . . .

A weak-kneed, shy, timid little girl, I was brought up in Dowanhill, Glasgow, running along, bowling a big wooden hoop, and sharing a scooter with my older sister, Ella. My father had been killed near Ypres, in 1917, and mother was left to bring us up, two babies. But she had the right ideas. A professional contralto singer, she taught singing and voice production. Ella and I grew up with scales and arpeggios ringing in our ears, and deep abdominal breathing became a way of life. The right way, because getting more oxygen is the heart of the matter.

And there is the first step towards good health and successful running – getting more oxygen into the lungs. It's the everyday, all-the-time first step towards better physical performance, keeping nerves under control and falling asleep easily. When stepping out on cold mornings, I've trained myself to say, "It isn't cold at all", and take a big breath. It helps.

When Mother overstrained her voice and singing career and developed laryngitis, we moved away from the winter pea-soup fogs of Glasgow to Leven in Fife. Soon we were playing golf with a No. 3 iron and a mashie, spending Saturdays at the tennis courts, playing as much pontoon as tennis, and swimming in the sea every day of summer. Sundays were for family picnics on the links of Largo Bay, and gatherings of aunts, uncles and cousins on holiday. The smartest ladies were Eton-cropped, ukeleles strummed and we played rounders; or was it cricket? When teams were chosen, I was always last to be picked, and if there was an odd number playing, I was given away. The indignity haunts me still.

Rabbits scuttled among the thyme-scented dunes (before the advent of Sunday trains). But the dunes are quiet again; Beecham saw to that.

Leven Higher Grade School was fortunate to have a sports field, where we could play hockey on Saturday mornings in winter. The cows took possession the rest of the time. Buckhaven High School, where I went at 15, had no sports ground or equipment. "You're here to work", said Mr. Buchanan, the Headmaster.

And work we did, entering the Civil Service, Ella as an executive officer and I as a sorting clerk and telegraphist, passing through clerical and executive grades to reach the departmental administrative grade, having read Law at Edinburgh University. There were no grants; I paid my fees, bought books, thought examination fees were expensive at 25 guineas a group, and worked an 11-hour day. What a pity I didn't run as I shuttled from office desk to University classrooms and back again.

But those were long-skirted days of dignity, when I was carpeted by my senior officer in the Scottish Home Department, St. Andrews House, Edinburgh. My offence? I had worn, on a Saturday morning at work, the kilt of my family tartan, Robertson. My accuser was an Englishman.

Though I worked on the fourth floor, I seldom took the lift. Even then I sensed that exercise was good, and extra exercise better. I cycled to and from the office, down to the New Forest, across

Denmark and all over Scotland. Ella and I were keen members of the Youth Hostels Association, sometimes walking in the hills, sometimes cycling, swimming as often as possible, and enjoying cold baths at home.

War came, and as an Executive Officer I was in a reserved occupation, and had to stay at my post, also doing night and weekend duties. I had been helping to look after children at the holiday camps that were organised for the unemployed, in the pre-war years, and now took Red Cross Nurse Training. When I entered the terminal paraplegics ward of the Edinburgh Hospital where I was to report for duty as a VAD (Voluntary Aid Detachment) for the very first time, there were no nurses in sight. "Nurse", called a patient, and more loudly, "nurse". "Poor man", I thought, walking down the long ward, "why doesn't someone come?" At last, "You wi' the Rid Croass oan, ma boa'le." I relieved him of that, and found a staff lavatory where I could empty it. Later, I was shown the proper sterilising equipment for these. That evening, three of the bottles cracked due to my over-enthusiastic sterilising. It was such a relief to put my nose to an inch of open window in the toilet while the steriliser did its work.

A Ministry of Labour appointment as Deputy Manager of the Employment Exchange at Fraserburgh on the Moray Firth, meant going too far from my mother's home at Leven to visit her at weekends. When told the news by the Establishment Officer at Ministry of Labour Headquarters, Edinburgh in 1949, I burst into tears. "How refreshing to see some emotion," was her comment. I loved Fraserburgh so much I wept when my time came to leave. Such miles of sands, empty but for seagulls, and the bay at Banff where breakers came rolling in, held enchantment for me. Sometimes, after hours of working late, I would walk down to the beach with my staff. In the darkness the waves were navy blue, foaming like lace at our feet.

1950 brought marriage and a home at Grimsby, walking and cycling on the great stretches of sandy, samphire covered beaches and swimming. Homes at Sleaford (Lincs.); West Bridgford (Notts.); La Paz, Bolivia; Derby; Tynemouth; Acasusso, Buenos Aires, and

Winchester followed, with four children to fill our days. With the Diplomatic Group in Buenos Aires, of which I was a part in 1968–70, my husband being First Secretary (Labour) for Argentina, Chile and

Early days at Sleaford with Edward and Adam

Uruguay, yoga was the 'in' thing. One friend went to classes, hoping to slim her middle-age spread. Her daughter wanted to expand her bust. "How can one set of exercises possibly achieve both those aims at once?" I thought disparagingly, and opted for massage. That was pleasant enough during the session but that was all, so I tried yoga. My teacher, trained in Japan, was gentle and thorough. When I could keep up with the other two class members in performing the Asanas and Postures at my first lesson, and complete the session with a headstand, she was delighted. And so was I, to realise I was so flexible.

Yoga became a lasting study, and a delight, all eight levels. In 1975 I qualified to teach Hatha Yoga, the physical aspect and meditation, gaining a Distinction from the All India Board of Yoga. With my experience of running, I am now of the opinion that yoga is not enough for general all-round fitness. How can a philosophy and a science, evolved in the climates of India be followed in Britain without adaptation? So, in my FITNESS and DIET classes, I teach Yoga Plus. As many of my students are retired, I find that the blend, which can be adapted to all age groups, is working wonders.

2 Starting to run

In 1978, as I finished a Bachelor of Arts degree with the Open University, I started running. When my husband, Fred, had said to me, "You're old, I don't want you, you're past it," that set me thinking. All my life I've loved hills and dreamed of Mount Everest, icily remote, its snows pink in the dawn light, silver gashed with black in the moonlight. I hadn't dared spend either the time, or the thousand pounds necessary to go. If I was unwanted at home, I'd go now. Hunting through holiday tour brochures, I couldn't find one that actually went up Everest, not even a little bit. And I didn't come across one that went to Base Camp, though there are plenty of these today. But Ramblers Holidays, with whom I'd been associated as a Walking Tour Leader since 1949, had organised a tour to walk up the Dudh Kosi valley, the river that drains the Everest Massif. I decided I'd go and send off the deposit. Back came a phone call, "You can't do the Dudh Kosi Tour, you're too old." Was this to become a theme song in my life?

A week later, 'Ramblers' phoned again. "We've remembered someone who was both old and fat, and she managed Dudh Kosi. You're wiry, you can go." So far so good, but now I began to worry. Was I really fit enough to stand up to altitude sickness, walking through possible snowstorms, sleeping on mountain snows. Besides, I'd never slept in a tent in my life, and had some doubts about Nepalese mountain curries. The thought of whiteouts scared me.

Seeing recruits running and training for their basic fitness tests at the army camp at Worthy Down where I was working, gave me the idea that running must be good fitness training. It's a really lazy way to train – no bother about joining anything or booking a space. No equipment needed and any old slacks and tennis shoes stuffed with soles of thick foam will get you started. A smart track suit and proper running shoes, which, incidentally, could prove to be the best

Alexandra Palace – July, 1979

investment you'll ever make, can come later. So, at lunchtimes, I ran around the perimeter of the football and rugby pitches – all of three-quarters of a mile. Then increased until I was doing four times around without stopping, but at a very slow pace. I use the word running, because I don't like the jerky impression that 'jogging' gives, and the activity should be done smoothly, with an even grace. By now, I felt that I could face the journey to work, three-and-a-half miles over the Downs, mostly field paths. The thought of sitting down to do my job for the rest of the day was an added incentive.

Rucksack on back, with sandwiches and a change of clothes, I set out in the grey light of November at 7.30 a.m. to be at my desk at 8.30. The first few hundred yards were the worst, up a slope, joints like an unoiled wooden doll. Passing cars would give me a toot of greeting. "Lovely day," shouted a negro cyclist one snowy morning. As I went up a footpath between fields of winter wheat, I'd wake up to the beauty of it all; the freshness of the morning air, the smell of the earth and the excitement of pheasants whirring away from me, only a few yards distant. One morning, in the January snow, I watched two cock pheasants fighting, more of an exquisite ritual ballet dance. Partridges would run ahead. I envied them their speed.

Every day at lunchtime, I kept running round the sports field perimeter, or taught yoga to colleagues; then, as soon as the days were long enough, I ran home in the evenings. With lunchtime runs that was about nine miles each weekday. And when I visited the doctor on the camp, that was another two miles. Wet or dry I ran, because in the Himalayas, we'd need to keep going whatever weather came. A peaked cap was a necessity, cold rain or sleet on the brow is numbing. My Dunlop Superstrider shoes sopping wet several times a week, stood up to the constant drying very well. Track suit just got soaked and dried on the radiator. I came out glowing from cold splashes in a toilet. Five months of this packdrill and in April 1979, I saw Mount Everest. Making a dream a reality is breathtakingly wonderful. But I didn't see it by moonlight. I must go back again.

Two months after returning home, I still felt exhausted. Thinking of ways to combat this, I thought I'd try running again. And that was

Setting out for Everest – 12 May 1979 with gifts from British Cubs for Nepalese Cubs. By kind permission of the Southern Evening Echo

the answer. In the hot days of July and August, I plodded home very slowly, but a night's sleep put that right. The lassitude, and day-after-day tiredness was gone. So I went on running to and from work for another two years.

Sometimes, as I gathered wild rose petals and elder blossom for wine, I would think: "How I wish I could tell unathletic people how enjoyable this cross-country running is. I want to encourage them to do it too." That wish has come true in a manner far exceeding my wildest dreams.

When the first Gillette London Marathon was mooted, I dismissed the idea of applying to take part with, "That's for real athletes, not for the likes of me." But George Cheatle, a Dublin marathoner (who had been one of a group I had led on a Ramblers walking holiday at Soller and Puerto Pollensa, Majorca) wrote to say how much he and his wife had enjoyed it, and finished with the question, "Shall we see you at the London Marathon?"

They had told such delightful stories as we sat sipping our black coffees and brandies in the evening, that I thought to have dinner with them the night before the marathon would be a real pleasure. "And I can drop out when I'm tired," I comforted myself by thinking. "Are you going to finish?" Brigadier Bernard Fullerton asked me. "There won't be anyone there the morning after to record it," I answered. My expectations of myself were low, but perhaps that was a good thing.

3 Preparing for the First London Marathon

When my postman met me on the pavement and handed me my acceptance for the marathon at the end of January, I danced for joy. I sensed something of real importance in my life. And when I read that 12,000 people had been turned down, all my preconceived ideas were wiped away. I had to earn my salt, make a genuine effort to finish.

A change had to be made from my idyll across the fields. Marathons are run on roads, so my route to work, accurately measured by Major Clark, under whom I worked, was four-and-a-half miles. That made nine miles daily, plus extra at some lunchtimes, as I still taught yoga on the others. Saturdays were for shopping and housework, and on Sundays came the crunch, LSD – Long Slow Distance. If I couldn't cope with my carefully graduated weekly increase, then I wouldn't be able to finish the marathon. But I always did cope so I don't know why I worry so much, and still do, before a race. Perhaps that's why I do finish.

Food assumed more importance. Thoughts of keeping my weight down were dismissed; building up strength and stamina, without adding too much weight, had top priority. Breakfast previously had been All Bran with added loose bran and wheatgerm, with milk, followed by a lightly boiled egg, half a slice of toast, marmalade and tea. Now, it became porridge, the usual loose bran and wheatgerm, with golden syrup followed by an egg and a whole slice of toast. Lunch was now two boiled eggs instead of one, with two cheese sandwiches, and at least eight or nine apples (our garden had 40 apple trees). Anytime I was bored at work, I would eat apples, and I mean EAT apples; skins, pips, core and all. 'Eat what would grow if planted', is a good maxim. Of course I took my regular supply of Healthilife vitamin and mineral supplements, Vitamins B, C and E, soya lecithin granules and wheatgerm, all important aids to health. I ate all seeds, orange, tangerine, grapefruit and grape, chewing them as well as I could and not taking too many at a time. Perhaps they're an acquired taste, but if I know something is good for me I eat it.

Our evening meal was home made soup, with home made wholemeal bread and liver, bacon and onion pâté made with garlic

Starting training – photo by kind permission of David Rice-Evans

and the herbs that I grew, followed by meat, potatoes and vegetables. Then, banished to another room, for the family don't like to hear me chomping, I'd enjoy watching TV while I munched my way through a large plate of salad, chopped apple, carrot, Jerusalem artichoke, crisp celery and cabbage, and the main item, weeds from the garden. Most people neglect the very freshest source of Vitamin C and minerals, that lies closest to hand – weeds. Dandelion leaves, plantain, ground elder with parsley, lemon balm, mint, some sage, rosemary or thyme, chopped finely with a really sharp knife, make lettuce taste insipid. To counteract the rather bitter taste of the dandelion leaves, some natural yoghurt blended with mayonnaise makes an agreeable dressing that isn't too heavy on the calories. For a sweetener, desiccated coconut and a few raisins, sprinkled over the salad, are delicious. Sunflower seeds are excellent too. In our family, it's not chips but sunflower seeds with everything. As in life, variety is all important, for we don't know in which substance fresh vitamins may be discovered.

For training, I decided that my four-and-a-half miles road run to and from work, with a mile or two extra at lunchtime was quite enough for routine training. But I learned as much as I could from *Running* magazine, *Athletics Weekly* and from Bruce Tulloh's *The Complete Jogger* (Macmillan 1979) and tried to glean information from people I met. A stay-at-home housewife doesn't have any athletic friends, so I didn't glean much there. My training and exercising boiled down to doing as much as my prodding conscience could fit into my way of life.

An attack of laryngitis held things up, and stopped my training for three weeks. I'd done the Alexander yoga pose, tongue stretched out, eyes staring, neck and jaw clenched so often, in my endeavours to cure the sore throat, that my neck was swollen and sore. But it passed and so did my training time.

Road-running, I found hard and wearisome. My road was crossed by three bridges, and on the way home in the evenings, tired after a day's office work, the distances between the bridges seemed to stretch longer and longer.

Now I had learned about 'fartlek' from Chris Brasher's column in the *Sunday Observer,* that is, bursts of speed, interspersed with ordinary running. I dismissed that as impossible for me as I seemed to be running as fast as I could all the time, not that it ever was fast. My first long run on a Sunday was a near-disaster. I ran for three-and-a-half miles, popped in for a cup of tea and a comfort stop at the house of the friendly Jones family of Qualsinn, Stoke Charity Road, Kingsworthy, Hampshire. Back home again, with some doubling backwards and forwards on the country road to make the trip eight miles. But how my knees hurt! Why, oh why hadn't I stopped as soon as they hurt I reproached myself afterwards. Next day, still in pain, I went for medical advice.

"Lift kilo bags of sugar, two at a time, with your ankles," said my doctor. I did; one breath, one heave. But I persevered, 30 lifts at a time, three times a day, lying flat on the floor. This exercise is a wonderful stomach flattener as well as strengthening the adductor muscles that protect the knee cap. Before long, I was managing a dozen lifts per breath, and totting up an easy 50 lifts per session. This added up to one-and-a-half tons weekly. But I still asked for help if furniture needed shifting. *Running* had published an excellent sheet of knee exercises involving leg swinging in all directions, while standing up and lying down.

When being filmed for southern TV's 'Day by Day' programme, I was doing these exercises before the cameras with James Montgomery producing. Yoga followed, seated on the floor, a twist, boat and some squats, then I lay flat on the floor to lift my sugar bags. "Go on with every exercise for 20 seconds," was the cameraman's demanding request. When I came to leg-circling, the camera was very low and so was my neckline. "You were disgraceful, Mummy", phoned my daughter Vivien from Sussex University, "you let the camera look down your cleavage". I was delighted her natural modesty made her protest. That didn't upset me, but when I watched, as my legs opened to their widest to make a huge swing (I was trying my absolute hardest to do well) there, right in the crotch, were tiny white holes. Oh, horror of horrors! I shut my eyes and couldn't look at the screen. How unprofessional, how shaming, holes in my tights. Next day, still feeling ashamed, I met my office friends for our coffee break. "Holes in your tights", was the greeting. "Nonsense", said the most observant, "the little white bits were the metal press studs of your leotard, shining in the camera lights." We laughed with relief. Of course my crotch was well and truly covered by three layers of material. But for months afterwards, people still said, "You had holes in your tights".

Swimming was advised as an aid for sore knees, so I ran a mile to the baths, swam a mile, and ran the mile home again – after a day's work. Bracing knees was another important exercise, possibly the most important, as it could be done at any time I was seated or lying down. I literally did it day and night. Hold the knee rigid, heel stretched out, knee pressed down hard; hold for a count of five, relax for three, and hold again. In the train I'd do it off and on for the length of my journey. I still do it. Under my desk at work, I'd raise my knees and hold and press; pressing down hard against the sheet, if awake in the middle of the night; with a rolled up towel below the knees, if lying on the floor. Fitness is a hard taskmaster, but oh, the rewards are great.

Back to road-running again, and I found I could cope, knees were behaving. "I guessed you were training for something", said a friend whose house I passed regularly. "When I looked over the garden gate after you, you were out of sight." That day I'd hopped on a bus for a check-up with my doctor. "I can't run fast", I bleated. He didn't explode, quite. "You musn't try to run fast, you're doing fine as you are." But I did try, though no onlooker would ever have known.

That's an important point for anyone over forty and new to running or jogging, call it what you will. Pay attention to aches and pains, and don't hesitate to get medical advice. My first thought on getting up in the morning these days was, "What's going to hurt today?" Happily, it was mostly nothing, but it pays to be watchful. You have to learn to listen to your body.

Our medical advice from the Gillette London officials said we must not attempt the race unless we had reached a 15-mile run by early March. Conveniently, 1 March was on a Sunday, and I geared my

Long Slow (yes, very slow) Distance runs to reach 15 miles a day. "The same route every time?" a friend was horrified. I ran the road to the office (with repeats) because I knew the mileages exactly, friends invited me in for squash or tea, and there was a pavement for a good part of the way. The London Marathon route was slightly downhill at first and then fairly flat, so, since this was to be my one and only marathon, it seemed sensible to stick to the same kind of terrain. Downhill running puts a strain on the knees, and uphill tests the hamstrings, so I was anxious to avoid these conditions.

But there were advantages. "Run 26 miles", sounds alarming, but "To the office and back three times", was homely, almost a game, and that was 27 miles. I cut down on the 'comfort stops' and disciplined myself to run seven mile circuits, with a 15-minute break at home, feet up, for milk, spoonfuls of honey, and a change out of sweat-soaked clothes. Then, off again, whatever the weather. "I want to offer you your bus fare", said a kind old gentleman, when I was running, one pouring wet day. But battling against wind and rain is all part of the training, so I kept on.

Skipping ropes were kept handy, and used at odd moments. Sit-backs, press off walls and step-ups on the bottom two steps of the stairs were fitted in too. I lived and breathed fitness. "She cannot be idle, as she for a Bridal . . ." runs the old song. Was I doing enough? (I felt I could hardly do more) and was I doing the right things? Only 29 March would tell me.

4 Countdown to the First London Marathon

On 22 March, my training peak was reached, two seven-mile circuits on the Saturday, and three on the Sunday, making a total of 81 miles for that week. Mike Tagg (at that time of Reliance Sportswear Ltd) had sent me, as the oldest woman competitor, a pair of road racers and a Vigo athlete's outfit, blue satin shorts and silky vest. I was thrilled and touched by his thoughtful kindness. Running in road-racing shoes was a revelation to me. The Dunlop Superstriders had been first class for jogging across field paths wet with dew, but proper running shoes gave me that mystical magic experience, a 'Runner's High'. Now we know that at a certain level of training, endorphins are released into the bloodstream, giving a sense of euphoria, and dulling pain and discomfort. I only know that running those high mileages that weekend, in gusts of strong winds and driving rain, I was ecstatically happy. My years fell away from me, as loping strides ate up the miles. While running, I wasn't conscious of fatigue, that came later.

Next day, reading *Running* over breakfast in bed, for I'd taken four days off work to be rested for the marathon (so I thought) I was disturbed to read, "Anyone running 20 miles on the Sunday before a marathon is crazy". And I'd run 21. Yes, I felt tired, and ached all over. Next morning, I thought I'd make amends by doing exactly as the experts recommended, and went out running before breakfast. I tottered home, utterly spent, after three miles. Starvation running wasn't for me. Perhaps – no probably – a marathon wasn't for me either, though my media marathon was in full swing, TV and Radio commitments, press interviews and photographic sessions.

My diary of that week records:

25 March 1981 – Odd how clocks go faultlessly all day, and stop in the night just when you've a 6.20 a.m. train to catch. A hot sweating night. We made love about 4 a.m. then I began to remember a different athlete's views on this 'none for a week before a big event', 'none for a month before'. But Laurence Morehouse, who devised the astronaut's fitness training while in outer space, recommended: "Do it right before and you'll be OK." That's two conventions I've broken, running 21 miles a week before, and making love five nights before. A drizzly morning, so quiet. Odd how you feel you must greet everyone you meet with "Good Morning". On the station was the 'South Today' Nationwide TV announcer who would have announced me last night, had I been on the programme as planned. Just as I was getting into the car the BBC had sent for me, word came by phone: "Don't come". I felt it would be indelicate to speak to him at 6.30 a.m. Now, sitting in the train I wish I had.

I checked over the names of the group I am to be on the air with (I was on my way to take part in 'Midweek', 25 March 1981). Russell Harty, Roger Royal, Conductor of Eton, Sir John Colville whose late uncle was Secretary of State for Scotland when I was a humble Clerical Officer back in 1936, in the office of the Secretary of State for Scotland, 17 Drumsheugh Gardens, Edinburgh. Cataloguing the office library as an evening overtime job, and sitting at the Secretary's handsome desk one evening, I was working on my papers when Sir John came in suddenly, not expecting anyone to be there. He apologised profusely for disturbing me – while I was ready to scrabble up my papers and depart. He used his private bathroom and went. I never had the nerve to see if it was a complete bathroom, but I hope it was, to afford refreshment after frequent journeys from London. So there's a link.

Leslie Thomas: a dash to the library for the only book of his on the shelves *Virgin Soldiers*. "I should have read that book thirty years ago", I said to Fred this morning, having had, in true Scottish Presbyterian fashion, to depend on gleaning sexual knowledge from the Bible. *Virgin Soldiers* was innocently instructive and funny too. I looked forward to meeting Leslie. Soprendo, a magician: Ian Gardhouse, the producer of 'Midweek' had said: "We thought it would be interesting, a magician on radio." Maybe. And David Royle, who will sing, and Russell Davey, inimitable slanter of ordinary events into diamond bright witticisms. I see in the *Guardian*, we are 'Russell Harty's People'. Train empty to Farnborough, packed now. Hardly room to turn a page, so I'll turn a blind eyelid.

London is grey and chilly with a windswept look. I remembered the growing excitement of arriving by train in Edinburgh and Glasgow, as a teenager. Cities, with their office blocks represented interviews, colleges, careers. Perhaps my radio interview will be on the same lines.

At Broadcasting House, Roger Royal joined me in the hall, and we went down to our Assembly studio together. He laughed and chatted in the friendliest possible way. Coffee came in plastic mugs, a dozen or so people all talking, all very 'Establishment'. Russell was there, in shaded tinted glasses. He took them off halfway through the programme.

After introductions, we went next door to our studio and sat at a big table, each with an individual microphone; Sir John Colville on my left, Russell Davey on the right. We were given the order in which we'd be questioned and told, "Feel free to join in at any time". I spoke with Sir John of the incident at the office of the Secretary of State for Scotland and he laughed. "That was my uncle; he would have been a hundred now." That brought a realisation of the passing of time home to me. Just because I hadn't seen or thought of Sir John Colville for forty years, I imagined him looking much the same as he was then.

Today's Sir John, a fascinating raconteur, spoke first. He was Secretary to Winston Churchill during the war years, and one-time Secretary to Princess Elizabeth, a friend of everyone worth knowing. Then came Russell Davey, whose account of the week's 'trivia', his own words, was exquisitely funny. His notes were written on a half sheet of A4 paper, the words so close together I wondered he could read the thick nib writing. He gives life another dimension. To see so much humour by giving everyday events a slightly incongruous twist, was richly funny. "You could change people's personalities", I told him, and decided to try and emulate his light-hearted approach to life.

Leslie Thomas, our Birthday guest and celebrated author, followed, talking of the birthday party he gave as a boy of six. Having invited his friends to sit in his council house garden, bringing their own plates and mugs, he then solemnly handed out single cubes of a chocolate bar and filled the cups with water. The guests sang 'Happy Birthday'. It was a real party. Life in a Dr. Barnardo's Home wasn't much different – you got an egg on your birthday. It's the thought that counts.

Soprendo, in a card trick, predicted the card selected by one of the guests, the seven of clubs. "Look at my advert in *The Times*," he said, "and you'll see my prediction". He was right – it was the seven of clubs. He really is a magician.

David Royle sang a delightful song, rather lost on me because I knew I was on the air next. It's strange that I should remember the content of Leslie's talking so much more clearly than that of the others. Perhaps because of having read his 'intimate' book, *Virgin Soldiers,* I feel I know him better than Sir John Colville, whose talk, erudite and packed with funny stories, escapes me. Perhaps it was the sheer volume he gave us. Leslie only gave a little, and simple, but it's remembered. Of course it could be an illustration of the kind of things a simple mind like mine remembers. Leslie, Sir John, Russell Davey very modestly, and Roger Royal were all talking about their own personal media programmes. They seemed to be doing whole series.

Russell had told me he would ask me questions after the musical interlude, so I could sit back and enjoy the others speaking. "I don't approve of jogging", he said, "don't like it. So I'll present you with that." "But I run", I countered. In the event he was very kind and didn't ask me any questions that were awkward. "Describe the route for the marathon and tell us more about this Tender Loving Care area", "I will, next week", I answered. When I mentioned starting running training because I wanted to get to see Mount Everest, Russell stopped me. "Just a moment, there's a sound of jaws slipping open, you wanted to get to Mount Everest?" "Oh yes", I answered firmly, "of course". "Hold on, take a little breath. You wanted to run to Everest?" It was all great fun with lots of laughter. After asking about my accent, which is Glaswegian, he said: "You have Bolivian overtones in your voice." So off we went discussing life at 12,000 feet, bringing up a young family.

"Do you know?" he said, "this conversation is like a pilot flying blind. I thought I knew certain things about you but at the end of every sentence you open a tiny door to some new prospect." "Did she find emeralds?" asked one of the guests. "We found emeralds and diamonds", I answered, "in the beauty of the land, the kindness of its people; in being up at 19,000 feet, looking down on aeroplanes flying, and seeing for hundreds of miles in every direction as we made our way upwards in the eternal snows."

"Do you write at all, Madge?" asked Russell. "I write, but I don't get published." "I'm writing it down", said one of the guests. Russell chipped in, "Do you write as well as you speak?" "Oh you are kind. Well let's hope I do, I've got masses of manuscripts at home. I'm writing a book, 'Fun at Fifty, Sin at Sixty, Can't wait till Seventy'." Much laughter, confused voices. "Can you help her, you've a great pull with all the publishers." "Who has?" "You." "How do you know?" "I mean surely you could help her." "I think I will, after the programme." It was Leslie Thomas, and he very kindly gave me his agent's address. "Write to him and be sure you go and see him." Unfortunately nothing came of it.

Already the race marathon seems incidental to my own marathon, getting 26 chapters published. I emerged from Broadcasting House ready to soak up atmosphere. The laughing, bantering of such talented people, even for an hour, was an inspiration. But one eye was half blinded by a great red blob. I must have burst a blood vessel with laughing during the programme.

5 Last minute preparations

We had been told that during the marathon, traffic would only be kept off the roads for a limited amount of time, a much faster time than I could run. If pedestrians weren't allowed to go through the Blackfriars underpass once the traffic was running, I was anxious to see what alternative route I could take. Runners abounded on the Embankment, as I walked along. I asked one or two about my problem, but they must have been fast runners because they had no idea, it didn't apply to them. I did see a walkway by the river and was satisfied with that. A toilet there, was padlocked, with a notice, 'If closed, go to Farringdon Street'. I hoped they'd open it up in time.

A cinema advertised 'French Love, Swedish Playgirls'. The Trafalgar Cafeteria at Waterloo suggested 'Get fresh with a Tasty Bite.' Another Waterloo idea was 'See London from top to bottom, the Go Anywhere ticket.' Is this a new syndrome coming out of my eye? 'Biggs Battles to Stay Free' screamed the headlines.

Walking up Bouverie Street, along Fleet Street and into the Strand was intoxicating; huge cars swerving past, prosperous looking men. You could almost feel the wheels of business humming. London didn't look a depressed city, it looked thriving. But then, the earning power of that part of the city had always been high.

Next day was back to work, but no running. Chris Brasher, in the *Observer,* had quoted a famous coach, "Before a marathon, leave off running for five days; make yourself thirsty for running". That seemed pretty good advice to me. Phone call after phone call came for me, my section leader at work was very patient. Curtis Brown, the literary agents, and Penguin wanted to get in touch with me; and Ian Gardhouse, producer of 'Midweek' too. "You know", he said, "I have a feeling you could do a script like Russell Davey. Will you try it? Send it in two weeks' time. You could come on when Russell isn't on." This was all very thrilling but I still had to run 26 miles. Everyone

I read about in the papers seemed lucky. Actresses, politicians, authors, they could be famous without 'hitting the wall' (when glycogen and energy run out at 18 miles). But in my saner moments I knew everyone has their own brand of marathon to get round, with all sorts of 'walls'.

My diary continued: 'M-Day minus one'

Woke with the birds after a good (surprisingly) night's sleep. But no more calm. Tummy revolving with excitement. Got up at 7 a.m. and brought breakfast back to bed; porridge, loose bran, wheatgerm, syrup, two boiled eggs and two slices of toast, thick with honey. And best of all my favourite tea pot that holds five mugfuls. My philosophy is that if drinking tea while catching up with the newspapers (one of my delights) I'm not wasting time. This is a dangerous philosophy as regards putting weight on, for it applies to eating as well.

Feel sort of sick, but I expect I would have anyway. Are my knees always so creaky stiff when I go downstairs? Is that a new pain in my right knee? How many swallows make a summer and sneezes a cold? I mustn't, can't possibly, daren't have a cold. Our advisers tell us that running with one might prove fatal. (There's one Agatha Christie didn't think of. Perhaps it would have been more in Edgar Wallace's line.) Tishoo! Oh my God! I'm nervously excited right to fingertips. Must stop thinking about self.

If Ed or Ad or Viv or Steve were running this marathon, I'd be sick with anxiety for them. But since I'm doing it, I don't expect anyone to be concerned; it seems commonplace, just another job to be tackled. Last night, I was watching BBC's 'South Today', having fixed a Radio Solent interview for 11 a.m. on Marathon Day plus one, at Southampton, when John Shrewsbury of BBC TV rang from London. I turned down sound, and as our phone is in a corner behind the TV set, forgot about my TV interview with Jenni Murray, that was about to come on screen. So I missed it. Arrangements for Sunday's interview and help with directing Adam to find me on Tower Bridge to give me milk, honey and a change of clothes, was more important. Where one changes in modesty on Tower Bridge during a marathon, I'll find out when I come to it. After we'd arranged for me to be met at the Olivetti tent (shades of Agincourt here) and conducted to an 8.15 a.m. interview with producer Tony Gubba, we rang off. But not before John had said, with real meaning in his voice, "I want to shake your hand". I'm touched, flattered and surprised.

Running is something I've done for two-and-a-half-years – the marathon is just the same only more of it. Just luck, my being 12 years older than the other women, and people start by saying nice things to you. I feel sorry for the two men in their seventies who are running in the marathon, training just as hard, but upstaged by Bob Wiseman, the 78-year-old entrant – and me – getting the fun of the publicity.

Still haven't decided what to wear – so much depends on the weather on the day. Chris Brasher, my marathon guru via the media, has suggested long johns under athletes' shorts if the weather is cold. But that kind of outfit is so outrageously different from anything I've ever worn that I'm shy about appearing in it. But Damart have very kindly sent me long johns and matching top in a lovely shade of blue and my Viga satin shorts match. . . .

"Eat plenty of sweet stuff", said a doctor on TV last night. Sounds like infective hepatitis. Edward brought out the black molasses tin and I've been supping it.

BBC 'Woman's Hour' Editor, Wyn Knowles rejected my proffered 'Woman's Hour' talks. "As you've been on the air with Russell Harty. . . ." Why do I think people will want to listen to me?

Now I'm bringing out old newspapers from the potting shed, looking for Russell Harty's *Sunday Observer* articles. He really is funny. But having met him makes a difference. TV first, and Radio second, add a flavour to anything anyone writes, because readers can more easily identify. In identification lies attraction. "In dreams lie responsibilities", Kafka. So we marathoners' dreams of success (merely finishing, for me) force us to take on the responsibility of hard training – and I found it hard. I was doing the job, housework and family cares that almost got me down. Some nights, climbing upstairs to bed, I was almost weeping with exhaustion.

My left eye still has a great red ball in it. No, not a punch up, that 'Midweek' laughter. My doctor had said, "You feel it's the end of the world, but it's commonplace. Will take three weeks to go away. Carry a mirror when running, and check. If it's worse, stop". When the blood had taken the shape of a question-mark, and more significantly, hurt, I went to casualty at the Royal Hampshire Hospital, as no-one had checked, to my knowledge, that there wasn't some foreign body tucked away in the eye. Lying on a bed, with the doctor's giant-seeming fingers probing, I yelled – it took two nurses to hold my hands and stop me from preventing the doctor doing what was necessary.

Then I remembered yoga training (my life is all training) and took big breaths. "You lift your eyelid yourself." I did, and then the doctor lifted it in the same way. No trouble. And nothing in the eye either. Came home relieved, with nuts for extra Vitamin A.

"It's your photo in the paper", said a passer-by, "I wish you lots of luck." Popped into the *Hampshire Chronicle* office for a quick look. Yes, not exactly a flattering photo of me, but a charming one of the daffodils in our garden. Came home and had lunch in bed, and then started packing.

Made a pocket out of a nylon sock leg – it can be pinned on to anything I'm wearing. Athlete's tops and satin shorts have no pockets, or minuscule ones, but surely athletes need to blow their noses. And I might need money. "Carry nuts and raisins", is another piece of advice. Yes, raisins possibly. And a pound note, and Adam's address and phone number in case I'm bemused and can't remember.

I had written to Bruce Tulloh, via *Running* to ask, "Should I wear a rucksack in this marathon, to carry wet weather wear, sandwiches and Mars Bars?" In my application to run, written in November 1980, I had agonised over 'estimated time of finishing'. I simply hadn't a clue at that time, never having run for more than three-and-a-half miles. The sensible thing would have been to go out and run a bit more, but I didn't think of that. I just filled in the biggest time that I guessed the admission authorities would allow, and in went 6.30, to be smudged to 6.15 and messed up to read 6.00 – that is, if anyone could read it at all, by that time. So, survival for six hours in the open air spelled a good meal. I toyed with the idea of a ploughman's lunch, for the pubs would be open, or better still, fish and chips, if I'd pass such a shop. The safest idea was the letter to Bruce, and he wrote back in all seriousness, though he must have had a smile, that I'd be quite all right without the rucksack or its contents. That the rain wouldn't affect me, and there would be drinking stations along the way. I settled for spoonfuls of honey and a drink of milk from Adam, halfway around.

My diary continued:

M-Day minus one, 28 March:

Off at last, one rucksack, large plastic bag, granny-holdall-bag and handbag. And here I am, an 'old bag' myself, off to run the marathon, feeling at least trim in my red and white Relum track suit, white pullover and luminous yellow Nike Elite Roadracers. The train is just sliding past the road, the curves, houses of Springvale, and three bridges that I know so well, every gritty, puddly, splashy inch of the way. And I'm sitting comfortably, collecting my positive thoughts of banishing the horrendous alarm that the thought of running 26 miles brings.

"Would you mind not sitting opposite me?" I asked fellow passengers, who approached the empty seat. "I have to keep a bad knee moving." That seemed to sound more sensible than "must keep doing my exercises". As there were plenty of seats, no-one minded.

A friend had phoned me (telling him of the 'burst blood vessel' in my eye) he said, "Don't go near the medics. They'll be cautious. Go on running, but let Adam check your eye at the start and the middle of the race. He can tell you if it's worse." At least I needn't strain the nylon sock by carrying a mirror.

Fred drove me down to the station, and I'm now ruminating on the different outfits I wish I'd brought with me. Wish I'd included a skirt or black pants. "It doesn't make any difference to anyone but the wearer, what is worn. It's the running that counts."

Until then, I had had vague imaginings of the 7,000 starters spread out on roads in a regular column, like a huge phalanx of Roman soldiers. That anyone would come and watch didn't occur to me. And that there would be enormous differences in the times taken didn't occur to me either.

"What are the prizes?" a friend asked. "There aren't any", I replied, "it's the finishing that counts."

> Looking back, the training has been more important than the marathon. I feel it's given me confidence and a solidity (yes, all those eggs). The Media Marathon was another factor to cope with, but all part of the training game. London sparkles in the sun. Hope I do, tomorrow.

Registration at the Strand Palace Hotel. The Strand is milling with people carrying the bright yellow plastic bags given to runners with their 'goodies', a Biro that erases, a copy of *Athletics Weekly,* wads of info sheets and advertising leaflets for just about everything that a runner might want – holiday trips, I see there's one to Oslo for the 24 July marathon – running outfits for hot weather, cold weather, wet weather, track suits, enough different makes, sizes, styles and prices of shoes to make choosing a pair a mammoth operation, vitamin supplements and electrolyte drinks.

Downstairs the registration hall was packed but everyone was so courteous, smiling and quiet, even though there were children around. I walked around the Strand Palace lounge, marvelling that I was there, accepted as one of the crowd. "Any chance of doing my back? I pulled a muscle this morning." The physiotherapist giving free advice was in demand as she massaged and rubbed, "Just relax," she advised the questioner. "I'll need to do a thousand sit-ups," said a voice in the crowd. "It didn't pull, it went to almost y'know . . ." Did anybody know, I wondered. But I did feel, in that cheerful throng, that everybody knew more, and was more confident than I was.

Home to Barbara and Adam's house at Southwark, and a pasta evening meal. Then deciding what to wear next day, and packing a bag with optional extras. A hot night, and I couldn't sleep, tossing and turning, thinking of my doctor's words, "Anything can happen in a marathon." But 6.30 a.m. found me out looking at grey skies and wet streets. "There are going to be traffic hold-ups, Mummy, we'd better go on the motor bike." What seemed normal to Adam was scary to me. A picture of me skidding across the starting line, in no state to reach the finish was all too easy to imagine, and we went by car.

All London seemed to be heading for Greenwich Park, but we

arrived just before 8 a.m. in time for me to be linked up with Chris Lewis of the BBC at the Olivetti tent and taken to the security officer's caravan, to await my TV interview call. Rain was pouring down outside, as I sat with my feet up, sipping tea and feeling guilty to have the privilege of such comforts that couldn't be given to everyone. By now I was enjoying myself, doubts and fears cast aside, the ADVENTURE had begun.

6 Race Day (Sunday, 29 March 1981)

Clad in blue Damart long johns and jumper top, I joined Tony Gubba at the TV unit. "I feel like a little girl playing at marathons", I blurted into the microphone, "but my training hasn't been childish; last weekend I ran 14 miles on the Saturday and 21 on the Sunday." This wasn't boasting; my anxiety was to let the people who'd been turned down know, that even if I failed in the race, I had earned my salt. I'd tried as hard as I could. Remembering the 'Nonsense' poem from the *Weekend Book*, I continued, "Nowhere to go but out, Nowhere to come but in" and, seeing Tony's face crease into what seemed to me a look of horror, I finished with "And nothing to do but run."

But there was more to do, I had to find the 'belongings' bus and a ladies' toilet. Greenwich Park is a gloriously big open stretch of land, so everything for the runners, with crowds of thousands in the organisers' minds, was generously spaced out. One bus held all the ladies' gear, but where was a toilet, when the brick park building was locked? "No" the security officer couldn't help me, and the starting gun would go in minutes. Racing across the grass (yes, really fast at this stage) to the long row of Portaloos all marked MEN or GENTLEMEN, I was so far from the start that I didn't hear the gun, but by the shouts that went up, I knew the race had started. So another girl and I dived into the GENTLEMENS. Then we couldn't go straight into the start for there were crash barriers up, and crowds, perhaps thousands of umbrella-carrying people, lining the route. So we ran to the very back of the runners and joined in, and then made our way down the quarter mile of Park Avenue to the gates and the starting line.

It wasn't the start we'd expected. "Walk", said a loudspeaker voice, and after 25 yards "a slow jog"; then "Walk" again. So it went until we turned at the gates and began a slightly downhill jog, great banks of smiling, cheering faces to add to the thrill of one of the most memorable occasions of our lives. We'd taken six-and-a-half minutes to get to the starting line.

"Where are you from, love?" and a man's arm slid round me. He was from Derby; it was all very friendly, chatty and warm, in contrast to the cold wind and rain. A man on a penny-farthing wove in and out of the runners without colliding with anything or anyone. A convict in arrow-clad outfit and chains had us laughing. It was the matiest thing ever.

As I passed two miles, my right buttock seemed to lock in a spasm and pains shot down my leg with every step. This was an entirely new experience, but I realised instinctively that it stemmed from being cold. I had foolishly taken off the Damart long johns and was wearing tiny blue satin shorts, and cosy wollen jumper that I'd bought specially at a jumble sale, so that I could throw it away. It turned out to be itchy so that was thrown away faster than intended, and I was cold, through and through.

As we approached Woolwich, there were patches of green spread across the road. They couldn't be leaves from the trees – it was only 29 March. They were squashed green paper cups, strewn all over the road, from our first drinks station, where young army cadets, eagerly held out cups, "Take mine, take mine", as if by taking one, we were granting them a distinction. I forced down most of two cupfuls, and added to the roadway's, 'Thick as autumn leaves in Vallombrosa'. There was plenty of khaki in the onlookers here, clapping, calling my name and "Good Old Worthy Down" where, at that time, I was working as a Civil Servant with the Ministry of Defence, the Royal Army Pay Corps. Now this warmth of communication helped. "Up the Women", "You'll finish". "You're doing great", "Well done", and "Madge, Madge, Madge". Sometimes a voice would shout, "There she is"; sometimes it was "There's the old woman".

On the morning when I took part in 'Midweek', my son's fiancée, Barbara Bleman, a teacher of English at an Inner City London School, had taken her radio hoping to hear me before class began. "What's that for, Miss?" the class were eager for any diversion. "I happen to know the oldest woman in the marathon, and she's on the air shortly."

"Madge Sharples", chorused the class, to her surprise. I'm reminded of how the day I started Teacher Training at Newcastle College of Education, began. The Principal met me on the entrance steps, "You're the oldest student in your year", he told me, "you're the oldest student ever to enter this college". "Distinction at last", I answered. Here it was, happening again.

The marathon route made a detour round a pleasant little open space where the *Cutty Sark* was moored. Considering that I was near the back of 7,055 runners who started, it was a muddy, slippery walkway, by the time I reached it. And my leg was giving me teeth-clenching pain. "When she's not running", I overheard two old dears say as I pattered cautiously past, "she's a lady". When my sister and Scottish relatives, the Reg Popes at Ceres, by Cupar, Fife, saw my slow progress here, on television, "She'll never finish", was the comment.

The shopping-centre streets were thickly lined with onlookers, cheering wildly, and to me, wonderfully. Past industrial parts, they were few and far between. One man gave me a narcissus, on a very dull stretch. Then we ran through a small park. "Call that jogging", sneered some youths, watching my slow progress, as I wound my way round.

On we went, across water, on a wooden bridge. "They've changed the route", I thought, "we must be across the river now". But no, we were still on the south side. More loo trouble; nothing and no-one in sight on some waste ground, some runners following me far behind, but huge sewer pipes laid ready to be dug in. I climbed in and put one to use. Traffic was running, as we reached built-up areas again, and the British Airways 'sweeping up' bus came round, the driver going very slowly past me with an enquiring look. Thumbs up, and a definite shake of the head for him; but we laughed to read on the side of the bus, 'British Airways Take Better Care of You'. Those who had given up, were seated comfortably inside waving to us. I would dearly have liked to have gone in the bus just long enough to hear their stories of what had gone wrong, but that's something for another occasion.

"Get off the road", a voice was bawling at me as I ran down at the side of a busy road with barricades between me and the pavement. We were nearer Tower Bridge now (I'd been thinking that for the last hour) and there ahead of me were Adam and Barbara. Out came the runny honey, and Adam spooned it into my mouth like a professional coach. Or how I imagine a professional coach would. Barbara was almost dancing in her excitement. "Are you going to finish?" asked a bystander giving me a look that had doubt written all over it. "Of course I am", I almost shouted, though deep down inside I felt doubtful too. But I knew that as long as I was conscious, I'd keep going. Adam waved the bagful of clothes I'd packed so carefully. Wet with sweat or rain, it didn't seem to matter any more, I'd go on as I was. "The race has been won", said Adam, gently, "Did you know?" His smile seemed to say "Is it worth your continuing now that you can't win?"

It was a little bit depressing to hear the shouts of the crowds and see runners streaming past, below Tower Bridge. They seemed to be running so easily and fast. I faced off to follow them round the Isle of Dogs. At a first aid post, I was given a cup of hot tea and a comforting rub for my leg. The warmth, both in and out, did me a world of good, for, dutifully drinking cold water and cold electrolyte fluid at every drinks station, I was getting colder and colder . . .

A thermal blanket helped that, and I came out, renewed. The second half of the run, leg pain dulled to a constant throb, seemed easier. My pace was slowed of course, and knees were beginning to ache, but there was no lip-biting pain. When crowds were sparse on the Isle of Dogs, a policeman cheered me on with his gasp of admiration, "Second time round!" Drinks stations had packed up now, but out came ladies with pots of tea and jugs of milk. How good that hot tea tasted. One group of ladies was watching; up went their skirts, and they performed a very good line song and dance 'Knees up Mother Brown'.

A voice came from behind me "I hate to tell you this, but I'm going to pass you", and a young man ran on laughing. I wondered why (when he could run with such energy there) he wasn't miles ahead.

Suddenly there was a 20 mile sign. That raised my spirits. If I could manage 20 miles, then 26 and the finish was a possibility. I could dare to hope. We were still passing through totally unfamiliar, almost empty streets, when a huge banner hung above our heads, right across the road caught my eye. 'Champagne and Fresh Orange Juice for Marathon Runners.' I was in time for an inch of soda water, but that was welcome. The novelty of passing through St Catherine's Dock and round Tower Bridge Hotel was refreshing enough to carry me on, until I reached the Embankment. To see Big Ben in the distance was a thrill, to be near enough to read the time was ecstasy.

The crowds there were out for a Sunday stroll, then they'd realise we runners were part of the Marathon, and excitement rippled along, smiles and shouts and cheers. One man kissed me, lots held my hand as I ran by, and some gave me flowers. Aches and pains were forgotten, almost. Crossing the busy Embankment to get to Birdcage Walk seemed a problem, among the streams of traffic, but a young man ushered me across. "I've left a wife and baby", he said, when we reached the other side. "I'll take over" and another man guided me round Parliament Square to the Walk. From there, it was a simple straight plod on to Buckingham Palace, but oh, how unending Birdcage Walk seemed.

No traffic now, and the crowds were cordoned off. I slanted across a wide open space by the fountain, to round into the final straight as a tremendous roar came from the crowds. "Madge, getting as many cheers as the winners", said the media. What felt like a youthful sprint into the funnel, was shown by TV to be a round-shouldered jog, but I was smiling, deliriously happy.

A lady leaned forward and tore my computer strip off my number. This was 'it'. I'd finished. "Here's your medal" and a small grey medal was pressed into my hand. "Take two, you deserve them". My time was 5.28.12. "You've to move on now", she added gently, for I was standing still, comprehending the momentous thought that I'd finished. Down another funnel, people taking snaps all the way, to a horseshoe of camera enthusiasts waiting for me. Adam was standing with Tony Gubba by the TV camera, ready to interview me. "How do you feel? Are you in pain?" "Oh, knees aching a bit, but I can still do 'Knees Up Mother Brown'." "Will you run again?" "Yes. . . ."

I wanted to find out what the tender loving care area was like, so, when Adam went for the car – and he'd brought me a flask of coffee and a thermal blanket – I went to a first aid unit. A lady put Vaseline on my knees, but this wasn't quite what I'd expected. Later on, I saw the tender loving care area on TV, and wasn't surprised I wasn't taken there. While I was bubbling with gaiety, the poor victims of aches, pains and blisters were prostrate under blankets, some writhing in agony. Ten had been taken to hospital.

Ian Wooldridge wrote in the *Daily Mail*:

> Back on the Embankment, they were still running or walking amid traffic now, for the streets had been re-opened. Among them, a 5ft. 1in. tower of defiance, was Madge Sharples who pattered on with tiny strides while explaining that a cup of tea at a St. John's Ambulance Post ten miles back had miraculously cured left buttock cramp. Mrs. Sharples is the wife of a diplomat, mother of four children aged between 20 and 28. She epitomised the long tail of a comet affair called the First London Marathon that roused a great capital city from its apparent deathbed, caused a million people to line its streets and restored sport to a genuine grandeur.
>
> It was a remarkable day – few; but a brash visionary named Christopher Brasher – believed it was either possible or even desirable. It was a brilliant success from the moment, on the Meridian Line at Greenwich, that a 25lb wartime field gun set in motion a softly padding exodus of 7,055 runners of whom probably no more than three had a genuine chance of winning over a distance of 26 miles and 385 yards.
>
> There were Australians, New Zealanders and Americans. There were Norwegians, Swedes and 26 Finns. There were so many others that it took six-and-a-half minutes to get them all over the starting line and all of 56 minutes for the entire field to pass the *Cutty Sark*, becalmed now in a dock only six miles away.
>
>

A hot bath at Adam's home was heavenly, then quickly into clothes to watch the race on TV at 4 p.m. It was a fantastic sight to see the river of bodies all in different colours streaming out of Greenwich Park Gates. And the loveliest part was how the two leaders, 21-years-old Inge Simonsen of Norway and American Dick Beardsley, 24, decided with a wink to end together with clasped, raised hands. That epitomised the emotions of the day.

Start of the Chelmsley Wood – determined to be warm and dry

7 Running at Chelmsley Wood

My original intention had been to take part in the forerunner of all people's marathons, The People's Marathon, at this time in May 1981, run at Chelmsley Wood, Birmingham. John Walker, the organiser, has made this race an epic. He had welcomed my application to run and asked me to come early, to take part in an hour long phone-in on the Friday before the Sunday race, on BRMB Radio, Birmingham.

Most of the questioners wanted to know the best vantage points to see the race, and there were some medical problems. (No, there weren't any ladies my age to compare notes.) After the questions and answers, we had a glass of wine with the radio station staff and all the delights of Birmingham shops were mine to explore. An assistant manager at British Home Stores recognised me and called a colleague, to my surprise and delight, and we enjoyed a chat about running.

Coventry – where I spent the night with my cousins, Elsie and Angus Bell, at Waverley Avenue – was a magic city of pink cherry blossoms. Their house lay on the edge of the Forest of Arden where I ought to have been trying out a gentle jog, but in the six weeks since the London Marathon, my only activity apart from working at my office desk, and housework at home, had been going to work by car with a friend, Ron Garwood (also working at Worthy Down) and to hospital by taxi. I was getting ultra-sound treatment for my damaged hamstring and had been cleared by Mr. Robertson, the surgeon of Southampton Sports Clinic only three days before the Chelmsley Wood Marathon. I was quite clear in my mind that running in a marathon for me, was out.

The day before the race I joined Ramblers Holiday friends, Basil and Alison Jackson at their Birmingham home. Of course I'd enjoy a night out with them and their neighbours, Leon and his son, at a very special country pub. Of course 1 a.m. found me tucking into coffee and supper – I wasn't going to run all the way.

But I wanted to see the start and felt conscience free at the thought of dropping out, after a couple of corners. After all, I'd been getting hospital treatment (for the first time in my life).

Starts are always exciting and this one was so well organised, it seemed to blend everything together. We registered in a big marquee on the day of the race, collecting race numbers and goody bags there and delicious sponge cake and fruit for us to eat on our way home, but more of that later.

We ladies had to make our way to a rather distant school changing room, on a vast complex of playing fields and open grassy spaces, but Leon was a real help carrying my luggage. Belongings were left in the open, a huge area of bulging black plastic bags, a fascinating sight.

A band was playing now, and drum majorettes in pink and white high-stepped smartly before the start, as if to provide a contrast in style. They marched cheekily, so erect, so precise in their movements. We stood waiting, swaying to the music. It was a perfect start, boom, and off we went straight forward, no gate to negotiate, no awkward turn to get round, and that describes the whole race – straightforward.

This marathon, I was determined not to be cold and was well prepared and wholly relaxed in my usual running clothes: Damart top, long trousers and plastic rubbish bag on top, for it was raining. I was going to do a couple of corners and no more. We started off, running through housing estates of pleasant modern houses – to my surprise bystanders were shouting "Madge, Madge" – there had been a piece in the local papers about my London run. Every corner brought a fresh vista of onlookers, so I kept on running and thinking, "Well, I must be looking my age if they know I'm Madge".

At two miles my groins began to hurt, but the rain had stopped and we were running down lovely country stretches; at one point, we ran down one side of a dual carriageway, the air heavy with the scent of gorse and broom that lined the road, while the 2,400 other runners (who were about two miles ahead of me) had turned and were coming back on the other side. It was a two-lap marathon. This meant a greater percentage of back-up help per mile, and was an added bonus for spectators.

I must confess for a slow-coach like me, it was a thrill of a lifetime to run past the 2,400 who were calling out greetings as they came back on the other side of the dual carriageway. The invalid chair boys were Trojans, making good time. One darling man ran in a splendid snow white tutu that fitted him like a glove, another hero was in a kilt and it was a real heavy thick 'six-yarder', soaking wet, in the rain. A Viking passed, golden horns pointing the way, brandishing an axe. Two men carried huge horses' heads, some deep symbolism there, but they ran like Greek gods – that was the beauty of this marathon route, we runners could see each other in motion.

In London, the leaders were so far ahead, even as I went over Tower Bridge and they went under (by the Tower Bridge Hotel) I could not see the fast runners to appreciate the sheer beauty of the human male running (the easy stride, erect body, smooth rippling of muscle, a joy to watch). It is thanks to people like John Walker and Chris Brasher and all the thousands of hard-working unpaid helpers, that we lesser mortals have been able to watch and actually join in this marvellous expression of joy that is marathon running.

A Southampton boy, Adrian, was running with me and we were joined by a lad on his bicycle, Chris Tysson, "Can I carry your wet things?" he called to me, and I, very happily, handed them over. Later on, when it rained again he gave them back, I wore them and then, heavier than ever, he took them back again. Cyclists aren't allowed to ride on marathon routes when the supervision of the police is complete, but they turned a blind eye to Chris. He would win a slow cycle race any day, because he had to cycle so slowly not to be dashing away past Adrian and me.

Here is an extract from my diary written at the time:

> Since the book I'm writing is 'Fun at Fifty, Sin at Sixty, Can't Wait till Seventy', I'd better confess. I didn't deserve all that wonderful cheering that greeted me, as I ran in at the finish, and the superb gesture from a gentleman who rushed out and poured a whole bottle of gorgeous foaming champagne over my ecstatically, happy head.

> I had only got round the marathon route once, so that was only a half marathon. As I said before the London marathon, "Nowhere to go, but out, Nowhere to come, but in". There was nothing for me to do, but run after the man in front, so that's why I found myself running in to the finish. I just went along with what was happening. When the first man passed me about ten miles out, I realised he would probably be the winner. He was soaking wet with rain and sweat, and ran past me, fast. Later on, to my delight, runners stopped, put an arm round me and asked: "How are you Madge?"

Since I finished in 2 hours 59 minutes, these were sub three-hour marathon runners, and for them to delay their finish to chat to me and encourage me and keep me going, was a marvellous gesture. Runners are wonderful people. Another thing that helped me on, was a shout from a lady outside a pub, "Want a drink of sherry?" and she came running down a slope at my enthusiastic "Yes", and gave me a tumbler full. Oh, that was good, and here I was, running in to champagne, unfortunately although I tilted my head, I only got one or two drops, but I'm sure it did my hair good.

Then we queued up and I was given a medal which, I ought not to have accepted. Alison and Basil met me and were so kind after I showered, and dressed. It's a lovely marathon when there is a hot shower waiting for you. After that they drove me into Birmingham station. "I'm proud of you", said Alison, kissing me. I was delighted.

On the train, munching my cake and writing up my diary, writing articles for the local papers (I never heard if they were published or not) but at least these freelance articles give me more to write about now. Here's one:

> If you're wondering if you would like to have a go at next year's marathon, of course you can. And NOW is always the best time to start preparing. You can begin in bed too. Set the alarm five minutes early and start the fun by stretching all over; separate your toes like fingers; curl them and stretch them; stretch out your heels, so that your legs are stretched hard against the sheet, them revolve your ankles first one way, then the other. If there's any crackling, you ought to do this more often. Knees, brace them down hard, heels

pushed out, toes pointing to the ceiling. Do this knee bracing to a count of three, hold for five seconds, relax for three, push down and hold again for five seconds and continue to do this at odd moments when you are seated throughout the day.*

Fingers, stretch and separate, hands revolve in all directions, fold each arm at the elbow and stretch upwards, elbow pointing at the ceiling; you can feel the stretch right down to your waist and your waistline will diminish. Then widen your shoulders, separating shoulder blades, and pull them in; do this several times, this prevents dowager's hump, that ugly fat on the back between the shoulders.

Now you're ready to get up and start the day. Tiptoe to the window to open the curtains or pull up the blind, walk back to get dressed on your heels, walk on the insides of your feet and then the outsides, and during the day, walk as often as you can bare foot or in stocking soles.

While breakfast is cooking, slip outside and run on the spot preferably on grass, or on a thick door mat. Only run until you are slightly out of breath; the eggs should be ready by about then and when you do the same tomorrow and the day after, you'll surprise yourself. I like to think of lots of Chelmsley Wood housewives in pretty housecoats bobbing up and down by their back doors and perhaps the smell of burnt toast hanging heavy on the air.

Before you start jogging it is best to get your muscles in trim if you haven't played much sport for some years, and you'll benefit by having a slimmer, trimmer figure. The last race I won, or even ran, was for the under tens at a Sunday School trip back in 1924. If I can run with the threat of arthritis hanging over me for the past 20 years, any one can do it!

*Before the London marathon, I was so anxious to strengthen my knees by doing this as often as possible, that I asked people on the train not to sit opposite me so that I could carry on doing it. I must have done this exercise a thousand times, because running is not something to be treated lightly. It is a job to be tackled systematically and persistently. You've seen the glowing health of the runners, the fun and companionship, it can all be yours too.

8 Andorra

One of my rewards that spring of '81, was an invitation to present the Trophy for Services to Sport in the southern region, at the Sports Council Southern Region Sports Awards lunch at REME Officers' Mess at Arborfield. Mrs. Audrey Crisp (the Brackness Archer) won that award, and I had the honour of being introduced to the big gathering by Ron Pickering, to make the presentation of a very handsome silver trophy. It gave me a warm glow when, colonels, passing through the Mess, came up to me, "I want to shake your hand".

I began to get ready to lead a Ramblers Holidays group, in duty-free Andorra, where even the waters taste superb. Tucked between France and Spain, its mountains rising to over 9,500 feet it is a perfect place to walk, scramble and glissade among the snow scarred peaks, plunge into cascading torrents and linger in sheltered valleys, lush with narcissus, tiny daffodils, anemones and deepest blue gentians. It's a land of mule tracks, but now civilisation is bulldozing its way in, making new roads up to the ski slopes and placing tall hotels and blocks of flats unexpectedly on mountain sides, but there are still many lovely valleys and slopes.

The group I was leading, 14 of us, had flown to Perpignan and driven in a comfortable bus through the valley towns of Escaldes and Andorra la Vella, hot dusty ribbons of traffic and shoppers, on our way to the cool, pure mountain air of Encamp. From there I hired a bus to take us quickly up to the mountain valleys, where we could start walking and enjoying the flowers from the first step. In two weeks' time, we met only one walker in the high valleys, an Englishman (naturally) with his dog, but we did meet two runners. I was relaxing over a chilled dry sherry in a pavement café in a village near Encamp when I noticed an Adidas and a Damart vest and trousers on a fair haired young couple. "We road run in summer," smiled the Spanish husband, "because I teach cross-country skiing in winter, we run about 20 to 30 kilometres each week-day, depending on the height we have to climb (and climb we must – for all roads lead up or down). No, there are no running clubs, we do it on our own."

In a land of no unemployment, little crime and a great surge of prosperity, perhaps most of the running is done to the bank!

Ridge walking is a delight, but sometimes to get high enough for that makes demands. The hill walker's maxim is: 'It's always steeper than you think', and when I don't like looking down, marathon training comes in useful. Just round that corner I tell myself when running (though in the Peoples' Marathon at Chelmsley Wood some of the corners were a very long way away).

On the mountains it was, "Just up to that rock . . ." Every day in Andorra, we went up a different valley; it's a wonderful land of flowers and valleys and exposed, very often snowy, mountain slopes. My greatest delight was plunging into the icy streams often under cascading waterfalls, the bracing effect of the icy water and coming out to hot sunshine was marvellous. After walking all day, enjoying those beauties of flowers, butterflies and vistas of more and more ranges of mountains, we would come down to a village where our bus would be waiting for us and enjoy our chilled sherry. The tiniest village always had their sherry perfect, dry and cool. Then we'd drive back to our delicious meals and comfortable hotel and in the evening go out and visit another hotel or a café.

One evening we met a Thames Television producer, Adrian Brown. He was passing through Encamp with a friend. "Would you like to see some folk-dancing", he asked me. I was with Dr. Harold Parks of Ross-on-Wye, one of our group. We looked at each other, "Yes, we'd be delighted, we'll join you in that hotel up on the left", said Adrian, "fix up a taxi, we'll be with you in half an hour". We sat there sipping more sherry until Adrian and his friend joined us and off we went to Escaldes.

In a big hall there was a concert of folk music and dancing; between the items on the stage, the audience rose to its feet, the stage magically lowered itself and we danced; then the stage would rise again and on would come the most wonderful Spanish Flamenco dancers. Adrian invited them round to join us for a drink while he discussed the possibility of their coming to England.

I had been swimming as well, plunging into the rivers which often weren't very deep, by myself or with Harold. He was expert at diving into lakes, and one day high up in the valley, I got ready to go into a river, white with foam, fields of asphodels in bloom on either side, a magic spot. We sent the men in the group on ahead, until they were tucked behind the woods, and then four ladies stripped off beside me (matronly, sensible ladies) and we rushed into the stream naked. Came out, flung our arms to the heavens, did a salute to the sun in yoga, splashed back into the foaming waters and out again to warm ourselves in the sun; danced about until the water dripped off. That was heavenly.

9 North Tyneside marathon

Back home and running to work again, but it wasn't dull by any means; friends kept writing to me, sending lovely cards, congratulating me on the London marathon. They had seen me on television and read what I had written about it in *Here's Health* and *Running*, and that started a chain of letters that hasn't stopped yet. I'm always battling with a tide of letters, which is a lovely heart-warming thing. Every morning is like Christmas Day. So I had to think again about what marathon I would run next.

North Tyneside was coming up on 12 July, so I concentrated harder on my runs to work, and tried to improve. Having lived at Tynemouth for three happy years, 1965-8, when my husband was an assistant regional controller for the North Eastern Division of the Ministry of Labour centred at Newcastle, I was keen to run in an area that I knew. Staying with dear friends, Thelma and Gordon Miller at Seafield View, Tynemouth was an added attraction.

Travelling up to Newcastle by train, the day before the marathon, a voice at my elbow said, "Nice to see you again". It was David Harvey, who had won the World Mastermind Championship Prize, when the competition took place in Australia. That was when our British Entrant, Fred Housego, came sixth. David's prize was a month-long trip to Europe with his wife, from their home in Auckland, New Zealand and we had been broadcasting on 'Midweek' with Mavis Nicholson some weeks previously.

In that edition, Lady Airey was the birthday guest. As she is a fairly slow speaker, and was telling us delightful stories about her father, my turn to speak came in the last few moments of the programme. Mavis introduced me, "Madge is in pink, she's lovely, she's in PINK". Then, "And what does your husband think of you running marathons?" I hesitated for a second, should I tell the truth? Should I make up an answer, or slide over the question and introduce another subject?

I told the truth exactly as it happened, "'Anyone can run a marathon, said my husband, running a marathon is nothing, 26 miles, 4 miles an hour, 6 hours, it's nothing'." Mavis didn't wait for any more, I was off the air at once, and soon we were going down the road for coffee and orange juice, Henry Kelly and Mavis making up the happy little band.

I had met David's wife, Fern, at the BBC and was intrigued by her name because I had once read an article in a Scottish newspaper about an Orkney family with the surname Fern, and thought what a lovely name it was. Twelve years after that, when I had a baby daughter, we called her Vivien Fern Sharples. And here was Fern Harvey telling me she was called after her Orkney grandparents.

As we lunched on the train, David gave us a running commentary on historical happenings in the areas we were passing through. He knew the name of every castle – his knowledge of British history is encyclopaedic. He has published *Song of Middle Earth, J. R. R. Tolkien's Themes* and *Dragon, Smoke and Magic Song*, both published by George Allen & Unwin (1985).

I was able to sample Newcastle's very fine new underground system, the Metro, and travel down to Tynemouth to meet the Millers. Over to the beach for a swim and a walk along the sands with a visit to Mrs. Carmen Stobbart, my sister in religion, who has since died. We had knelt together before the Bishop of Newcastle when we joined the Anglican Church in 1966.

For six months, we had attended confirmation classes at Tynemouth held by the Rev. Stephen Huxley. It was the regular habit of class members to visit a pub on the way home. Carmen was 'into' gin at that time and she introduced me to it. I used to drop in to see her at odd times in the morning or afternoon, thinking that this might lower her consumption of gin; but it didn't, it just increased mine.

I wasn't going to go inside her house, and with next day's marathon on my mind, I wasn't going to touch gin, but there was Carmen, in her seventies, as large as life and full of good spirit. Out came a glass of sherry, handed out to me in her garden. She had had treatment and dried out, when a friend, not knowing this, had brought her a bottle of whisky, and she was off again, on the whisky. But she looked lovely and was as hospitable as ever in her lovely home.

North Tyneside Marathon day, 12 July, 1981 was fresh, with plenty of clouds blowing around, but invigorating. Thelma and Gordon drove me to the start on the grassy links of Whitley Bay, close to the sea. All around were friendly greetings, and I was surprised once again at how many people knew me. There were even shouts: "Sports Personality of the year, we're voting for you, Madge, we're voting for you".

Instead of a gun, a maroon was fired, and off we went, over the grass and on to the road, up past a caravan park and up some long sloping hills. Running in new country, through villages, was a delight, now running with a girl, now with a man, sometimes with youngsters who weren't in the race. It all helped to pass the hours.

Twice that day, Thelma very kindly came driving along and gave me honey and glucose sweets. Between looking after her family and guests, and dashing out to find me, she certainly had a busy day, and I did appreciate the honey. For the latter part of the marathon, Peter Scott of Chester ran with me, his first marathon, and I was very glad to have his company and his help at road crossings.

Towards the end, when we came to a rise, heading eastwards, I thought, "This is the last rise, from here we go straight down to the sea". When it wasn't the last rise, and that happened three times, I was demoralised, and thought fiercely, "I shall never allow myself to be in a position like this again. New York Marathon, NEVER". But the fourth rise came, and we did run right down to the sea and straight along the promenade through Cullercoats, that lovely little fishing village, and on to Whitley Bay and the Links again. About a mile from the finish, Peter dashed ahead to finish under six hours (of course he had been slowed down because of me). He was very kind to wait until there wasn't a single road to cross, and plenty of people around to help me if need be.

Just over six hours I ran in, and there was Gordon Chester, the race director, standing with two beautiful medals ready for me. He had taken the cue from the London marathon. After photographs and a broadcast, on to the Whitley Bay recreation centre, with its glamorous swimming pool like something out of a Hollywood film. A swim after a marathon is the best possible finish.

A meal with Thelma and Gordon, and a drive to Newcastle to do radio interviews with a freelance. These ended up being broadcast in England, Scotland, Wales and Ireland. A friend was driving through Wales, when she heard me; then again, during her holiday in Ireland, and once more as she crossed England on her homeward journey. And I never heard it!

Up at 6 a.m. the next morning and back at my office desk at Worthy Down, soon after 2 p.m., not a bad time after running a marathon in the North of England the day before.

Now New York was lying heavily on my mind. I got the chance to have an operation for the relief of haemorrhoids, but that came on the day my daughter Vivien was going to graduate at Sussex University. I was so anxious to be there and see my darling getting her degree, that I cancelled the operation. Sadly the event didn't come off, she took her degree (BSc.) by post. Never mind, I was getting on with my training for New York, and another important event in my life was very close.

10 Retirement and a Fresh Start

On 4 September 1981 I reached the age of 65 and retired from my work as a Ministry of Defence Civil Servant with the Royal Army Pay Corps at Worthy Down, Winchester. I had decided to invite some people for drinks in the cricket pavilion at midday. It took quite a lot of time just inviting them, and then arranging what drinks to have and who was to serve.

I was determined to run to work on that day and set out very early and ran on the road, a beautiful morning, sunshine, blue skies. The press began to come out about 9.30 a.m. so the men I worked with were very kind and allowed me to go out and meet them, I ran here and there, passing this sentry and that (whilst being photographed) and these are some of the best snap-shots I've ever had in my life.

On the previous Saturday, I'd opened the Highcliffe Community Association Fête, and been presented with some gorgeous flowers by little Elaine Oram, daughter of the association's hard-working secretary, Mrs. Grace Oram. They decorated the cricket pavilion beautifully, but it hadn't been cleaned and midday party-time was approaching. At last a soldier came to sweep it out about 11.50 a.m., he thought the party was starting at 12.30 p.m. It was a scramble because I couldn't leave till I'd seen the place cleaned. Then I had to dash back to my office and change, I had bought a new jump suit, the very latest fashion, pale pink, that I wanted to wear for the presentation.

Everyone was gathered in the hall with the Colonel ready to make his speech, when Major Clark escorted me downstairs to listen to the Colonel's words. I had given my tape-recorder to colleague Ron Garwood, asking him to tape the proceedings but he had decided that he must be right beside us to do this, so we made a little triangle in the middle of the floor. I had given my camera to a soldier who was keen on photography, he came forward wanting photographs of the

Colonel and me; I was signalling Ron to slip aside , but he thought I was asking him to come even closer to be in the photographs, so we

Running to my retirement office party –
Photo by kind permission of the Southern Evening Echo

had a hilarious session of signals and tape-recording and photographs. I was probably ready to laugh whatever had happened. The following article from the *Hampshire Chronicle* sets the scene of my retirement:

Madge Sharples Runs on into Retirement

Retirement is not going to mean an easy life for Winchester marathon runner and fitness enthusiast, Madge Sharples.

Madge (65), who retired last week from her job as a civil servant at the Royal Army Pay Corps, Worthy Down, plans to continue to compete in marathons, lead trekking holidays in different parts of the world, write a book on keeping fit and pursue her favourite hobbies which include gardening, skiing, golf and dancing.

"My children have already told me that I'll have to go back to work for a rest," she joked at a farewell party at Worthy Down, which was attended by more than 80 friends and colleagues, including the Station Commander, Brigadier Bernard Fullerton, and his wife.

"I feel as if I'm leaving school – I feel 16 not 65 . . . I plan to run in marathons in different places around the world for as long as I am fit and healthy", she said.

For the last three years, Madge, of Andover Road, Winchester, has run the four-and-a-half miles to work and back. Next month she is to compete in the New York marathon and is presently looking for sponsors to raise money for the Wessex Body Scanner Appeal. She is also helping to organise the Winchester Marathon which has been set for 14 March next year.

But she also plans to concentrate on writing and travelling. She is currently working on a book about fitness and will continue to travel as a group leader with Ramblers' Holidays.

Born in Glasgow, Madge obtained a Diploma in Public Administration from Edinburgh University in 1949 and two years ago graduated with a B.A. degree in Arts subjects from the Open University. She has also lectured in English literature, cookery, nutrition, keep-fit, and has successfully brought up four children.

Madge joined the Royal Army Pay Corps in 1975 and on Friday in last week she was presented with a gold necklace and ear-rings and a book by Colonel Ray Crompton, the Command Paymaster, on behalf of colleagues at the Pay Office. She now believes her most important job is to attempt to encourage people – particularly the elderly – to become fit and get more fun out of life.

She will certainly be missed at Worthy Down. Mrs. Pamela Fullerton, wife of the Station Commander, said: "Madge has set an

> example to us all, not only because of her running, but because she is actually doing something worthwhile with her life. Worthy Down will not be the same without her".

By kind permission of the *Hampshire Chronicle*.

It was a lovely time and everyone was so kind, giving me a beautiful gold chain necklace with matching gold ear-rings and a Roget's *Thesaurus*. I had been asked what I would like for my present from my office colleagues, and not knowing how much money would be raised (also aware that I had only been a couple of years with that section of the RAPC) I wrote down a choice of three things that I thought gave a wide range of expenditure. Instead of getting one of the three, here were all three – and a huge card of red roses, signed by so many people. I treasure it still. When I went over for the drinks to greet people and chat and pose for photographs, more newspaper reporters arrived, I was really spending more time chatting with them than with my guests. It was a most perfect day of sunshine and we could see for miles from the cricket pavilion. A lovely memory for me, and I hope for the others too. That was 4 September.

On the 6th I set out to lead a walking holiday for Ramblers Holidays in Normandy. Our destination was Thury Harcourt on the river Orne. It has an interesting history: the Vikings had come in their long boats up the river as far as Thury, whose name came from Thor the god of war.

As time went on the original landowning family became impoverished and the estates were bought by the wealthy family of Harcourt. The town then took the name Thury Harcourt and the lord of the manor became governor of Normandie and a Duke. To house administrative personnel for his duties and 31 military personnel, he had to add a large wing to the chateau, and that part still stands on the rocks above the road leading down to the river, while the château is no longer in existence. During World War Two the Duchess of Harcourt, a very religious lady, with sublime faith in God's protection, would not allow any valuables to be removed from the château for safety. The Germans had been in occupation of the château only for a month, and had actually lived in it only for a week before 30 June 1944, when the Stafford Regiment (59th Division) shelled the town and razed between 70 – 80 per cent of the buildings.

The Duchess still blames the caretaker for letting the Germans into the château. By a 'miracle' only one or two shells hit it, but as the Germans moved out they set it on fire, burning treasures which included (in its library) a priceless collection of manuscripts relating to the trial of Joan of Arc.

During the occupation life went on fairly normally for the townspeople of Thury Harcourt. When I mentioned a Fifth Column, this was indignantly repudiated. "Yes", said my host, a freelance journalist, who is researching the history of the area and runs the Syndicat d'Initiatif of Thury Harcourt, "there are stories of spies, collaborators, of followers of Pétain, of de Gaulle, of supporters of the Free French, but", he insisted, "these are only stories, they are not history. It is too early for that, we only know and remember with sadness, how families, friends, the whole country was divided." His own particular job was to arrange the transport of bodies from one district to another. Schooling went ahead normally. Young people went to University. But the tales of the unseen heroism of the people of Normandy are still unsung.

The Duke was paid government compensation for the loss of his château, but to the distress of the local people, instead of rebuilding, he invested the money in Algeria. He managed to pull out of that country without loss, and is now going ahead with plans for a leisure centre in France.

That was a lovely week, walking on the quietest of footpath tracks, tiny roads past farms, where sometimes they would give us cider to drink. Often we were up on the top of ridges, walking along eating apples, enjoying the views, and talking, talking, talking. Then we would come down to the river Orne and swim. One day, I remember, three other ladies joined me, I was in the river in my bikini and they came in, middle aged, sensible ladies, one was a doctor, one a dentist, one a mother of young children. They were bathing naked, long hair flowing down and they were beautiful. This was like a French

Impressionist painting, the sunlight glancing off the water, reflected the creaminess of their bodies and their hair floating in the wind. The slow flowing Orne and footpaths of Normandy had given us a tranquil week of freshness and peace – a contrast to my next Tour.

Walking above Soller, Mallorca

11 Sea and sun at Majorca

Majorca is a wonderful island for holidays; we spent a week at Soller and a further week at Puerto Pollensa. I was leading a group of 16 Ramblers Holiday-makers, all good walkers, a lot of them keen swimmers and very much into everything going on around them, in other words, very good company indeed.

The holiday plan was to walk as much as possible, enjoy the sun, the wine, the swimming and the company. We had one wonderful day on the mountains over 3,000 feet high, and walked along a ridge 2,000 feet above the Mediterranean to Valdemossa – memories of Chopin and Georges Sand. We lingered in the monastery cells they had rented (to the shocked disapproval of the local people) and sat on the fragrant south terrace among lavender and honeysuckle. Palma, its fine cathedral and fascinating little side streets of shops, was another delight.

One of the special features of life in Majorca is, on Sunday mornings to go to a bar, frequented by local people; we were in Pollensa, one Sunday, after climbing the steps to the Calvario, a wonderful viewpoint with a little church, and went down to Laborach for a drink and tapas. These are pieces of squid or octopus, tasty little titbits in dishes on the bar counters, that we nibbled as we sipped. Men were standing, six deep in the bar, singing the Saeta – religious singing originating in Seville. It sprang naturally from these men, their voices deep, trembling with emotion, for this is a part of their lives. They were led by a clear-voiced lead singer, his heart and soul in the music.

Alcudia made another good day, with its small Roman amphitheatre and many Roman remains, a whole city yet to be explored in depth. We went to a cave that had been used for storing grain in Roman times, and used as a shelter from then to the present day. It is now used as a night-club, decorated lavishly, furnished with most comfortable sofas and chairs, yet keeping the ancient rock roof and walls. Flamenco dancers came in and gave us a marvellous show, whether this was because we were in a cave the atmosphere was so right, I don't know, I do know they were first class artistes and I know that the dancing and the music, mostly guitar, throbbed our very heart-strings. We also had a chance to dance and we all enjoyed that.

There had been an International Festival of Folk Dancing in Soyer, and we arrived in time for the final grand evening. I rushed out and bought little cakes, dates, sherry and fruit juice, got tickets for everyone and shared out the food and drink.

You could tell the geography of the country the dancers had come from, by the kind of trousers they wore and their footwear. There were sheepskin-clad Sardinians and Italian dancers from Naples in home-spun grey clothes with very thick knitted socks. They danced with tremendous vigour. It was an enchanting evening and was repeated on the Monday night when all the tourists in the area were invited to a tourist evening at Puerto Soller, held in the huge football ground, surrounded by eucalyptus trees. This event was thrown open to the public, and we were given the most wonderful buffet meal. We could gather up whatever we wanted from stall after stall; every kind of seafood, delicious mussels, crab, different kinds of fish, as it was cooked. I couldn't make out what each one was; all kinds of pasta, paella and wines red and white. We could drink from the proper traditional clay wine-holder, when you hold it high above your mouth and pour your fill.

You have to learn how to do this, or it's likely to pour down your chin and on to your clothes, but it all adds to the fun. The array of fruit, red and white melons, apples, oranges, pears, peaches, green figs, was a feast and all by the light of flares with music playing all around us. We wandered round, tasting this, tasting that, huge sausages, some potatoes (I didn't have many of them) but I kept going back for more mussels, they were superb. Then we went to a huge arena where the dancers were going to perform again. After their performance, the public danced too, we were all dancing together. I found myself with a Sardinian with enormous shoes, but oh, it was so enjoyable.

Majorca is one of the most wonderful places in Europe for holidays, you can so easily get away from the crowded beaches and package tour hotels, if you want. Although I'm sure package tour hotels offer a very good holiday.

Here's an extract from my diary:

I'm on the Ciudadela – hot sunshine, French singing – a songmaster who sang the verses while we joined in the choruses. Photographs, the whole group assembled – and camera after camera handed to the photographer who almost toppled into the sea in his enthusiasm. So relaxed, friendly, happy, sun glancing on the water, fish voulez-vous? to everyone – an extra helping just dolloped on to my plate. Then fruit, coffee, brandy, is the sunlit water more enchanting? Clear to the bottom – 18 feet or so – we can watch the fishes darting, swarming, twirling, sun is hot on the rocks and we're in calm waters, Calamarta, after a morning of fishing. Letting out a long line, the boat rocking, I caught ten golden, delicious little fish. Somehow we sit down to eat fish, but catching it and pulling in the line does seem cruel, but I did it and dived off the boat into the waters of Calamarta. Sand below, clearest water above and tango music to keep our rhythm. The waves sparkled and splashed. We turned past tiny secluded marinas, private jetties, villas high on the hills, steps down through the fir trees and olive groves to the sea. It's the only time I envy wealth, but oh to live there in houses with balconies facing each phase of the sun.

But here I am, tanned and salted, refreshed and invigorated, laughing and joking with the French group on board. At lunch we sang, then came a tongue twister, different parts of the body to be named and slapped in a certain order. After four glasses of wine, fish, salad, melon, grapes, coffee and cognac, I was confused to everyone's amusement. "I thought I was going to be kissed", I said to my neighbour, when the song leader came and sang a special verse of the song for Margaret, I wasn't kissed, my face was rubbed hard with a wet towel, that was when my question was easily answered, laughs and kisses all round. Such an easy, happy, informal, group feeling; Claude, Marcel, Jan, swimming, joking, gazing at the marvellous changing cliff face and colours of the rocks as we passed. Cliffs up to 500 feet high, caves with stalactites dripping.

A few grebes dived and bobbed up as we passed. One light-coloured, long-necked seabird dived and we were out of sight before it surfaced. Chatting, smoking, enjoying the sun and wind, the men comfortably fat, yes, even the women and young ones so secure in their attachments were fat too. I thought the girls were pregnant until they appeared in bikinis, but no, it was just the generosity of flesh that to me is the ultimate in happiness. What a wonderful day, I nearly went to Ignatius, the boat owner, to apologise for not being able to raise a group to pay to come on board, when he came in his car to meet me and drove me through the town. "I haven't a group", I said, "and the French people who were going to come, haven't arrived, and I don't want to pay myself". "It's all right", he said, "come on". And I did. Now, sleepily drunk with sun and sea, all is serene – I can see yachts and hills clearly etched in the evening sun, how good it all is, so colourful, tasteful – and it's not over yet, I must train hard, work hard. Life is fantastic.

Ode to Madge – Ramblers Holidays Tour R.5316

Ten Ramblers set out for Mallorca
With hope, on a wing and a prayer
To meet up with a comforting Leader
And give themselves into her care.
Along came a species of Sharples;
A wee lass of sure foot and quick limb,
Enthusing soft Gaelic grace and humour
Ready to pander to their every whim.
She gave each, individual attention
To make sure every moment was right;
Bobbing up from her seat like a yo-yo
Ne'er getting a morsel to bite.
Her charges were all shapes and sizes –
You could say a right motley crew,
Posing questions like a judge in Assizes –
Is this spring water? and Where is the glue?
She guided them safely down mountains
With only an occasional lapse
And this she explained in fey language
Was due, to a wee crease in her maps.
One week of some splendour in Soller
Accustomed palates to mighty good food,
But on arrival in Puerto Pollensa
The awakening was exceedingly rude.
Eily's con leche was no longer caliente,

Hens laid an abundance of eggs.
Were two rolls each morning at breakfast
Enough for Mike's growing legs?
Janet complained **her** eggs were not frito
She hated them served in her hat
And had to manage on cheese and salami –
She had had quite sufficient of that!
The party pondered permutations of puddings
And let it quite go to their heads
When dear Madge wangled a dish of melonen
To send them all happy to beds.
In full sun, as they trudged upwards at mid-day
And Alison came out of the shade,
Madge encouraged with words of the Marathon
Crying, you too can all make the grade.
No Marie, you won't need your umbrella
Och aye, there's bound to be somewhere to swim,
I'll always lend out my bikini
To Cyril – I'm sure it looks better on him.
So Madge dear, with love and affection
Ten Ramblers wish joy where 'ere you may run
And give thanks for your care and attention
During two marvellous weeks in the sun.

Written by members of the group.

12 Training at Cobham

I was home on 3 October, with three weeks until I was going to run in the New York marathon. That was a time of anxiety. Was I doing enough training? Well I just had to get on with my letters and housework, seeing to things at home and the family and getting ready to leave on a running tour on Thursday, 21 October.

A marathon training weekend organised by *Running* seemed a good idea. It was to be held at the Ladbroke's Hotel at Cobham, Surrey. I arrived on the Friday evening, full of hopes. Was this to be the magic key that would give me the knowledge I needed to unlock my latent running abilities? It was a particularly comfortable hotel, and I appreciated making tea in my room after a leisurely bath. Then down to dinner and a talk by Don Shelley, at that time national marathon coach.

The team looking after us were illustrious names in the world of running. Sylvester Stein, publisher of *Running*, and a champion veteran sprinter, in his early sixties; Andy Etchells, editor of Running (and young enough to be my son) Bob Holmes, ultra-distance runner and writer, and Alison Turnbull, women's editor of *Running*.

My diary records – Saturday, 10 October:

Happiness is a runners' weekend. Total comfort, delicious food, like-minded companions and running. Don had given us a talk on the finer points of marathon preparation and training. Our aims should be:

- No short cuts,
- Daily Training,
- Get consistency,
- Put in a fair amount of mileage,
- Keep up a good pace,
- Get sufficient rest.

Weave these aims into your habits and make them part of your life. Don't stop to think, go on and do it. As you get fitter, your mileage will increase on your longer run, because you'll be running faster. Listen to your body, and let it dictate.

Seb Coe has a set schedule, but he can handle it. Carry on longer, when you want to do it, but if tired or injured, take time off. Don't look for excuses. After a marathon, take a week's rest, with only jogging. The secret of marathon running is knowing yourself – know the race and know yourself. Coe runs into oxygen debt – so he trains by doing so. Fifty miles a week is a good target to aim for. If you run a minimum of 50 for two or three months before a marathon, you'll run a race to the maximum of your ability. Book terminology is misleading. If there's a prize, it's a race. Jogging is a word invented to keep people from being afraid of running. It's all relative to individual performance; find what makes you improve.

We used to go out and run as many miles as we could, before science entered training. Jogging the day after a marathon gets rid of poisons in the muscles.

Start off at a certain level and learn to run on a regular basis before you train. Run your basic mileage for four weeks, then increase by up to 20 per cent, for the next four weeks. Run your furthest distance three weeks before the marathon. Then, reduce by 20 per cent to one week before, when you should not do too much. Build up the glycogen levels in your muscles and let the body rest. Do fast running for shorter runs. Push yourself up to your target, for your body gets used to such targets and can handle it. Learn to run when you're tired; twice a day is better than once; start tired and you build up.

Factors that a trained body demonstrates are:

- Fast running means maximum oxygen intake.
- Muscle endurance increases.
- Fatty acids are used more easily.
- Sweating ability increases.
- Heart beat decreases.
- You become a more efficient machine.

For training		*% total mileage*
Sunday	A long easy run,	30%
Monday	Short fast run, marathon pace or faster,	10%
Tuesday	Short easy run or day off	10%
Wednesday	Long run, holding back,	20%
Thursday	Short fast run,	10%
Friday	Day off or very short easy run,	5%
Saturday	Race or fastish run.	15%

Run a marathon first, and just finish. Then race a marathon, start slow and finish fast; it is great if you push yourself.

Use a training diary fully, recording time and place, weather, where it was, how you felt, what you wore. Keep a weekly mileage chart, and a monthly record of times. Weigh yourself weekly. Your optimum pulse rate should be 220 minus your age. Don raised a smile, "My pulse rate was 40 – a nurse ran off". "Sure that's why she ran?"

"Before a race", Don advised us,"you should only eat what will be digested fast. And that should be taken two-and-a-half to three hours before. Toast, with marmalade, honey or syrup, and plenty to drink". Ron Hill likes jam butties. Coffee or sugary drinks can be taken for up to an hour before the race, as caffein releases fatty acids.

Set out your target time, and break it down into five-km. splits. If the route gives five-mile points, then work out your times for these, calculate the right pace for you, and aim to finish all in.

Experiment with your pre-race diet, but make sure it's a full diet so that you are getting enough protein to maintain muscle strength and replacing glycogen lost on long runs. On the Wednesday before a Sunday marathon, you should be on maximum carbohydrate intake. After that, cut back, taking starches rather that sugars. A diet rich in carbohydrates needs extra fluids; you don't want to be dehydrated in the race. Brian Maxwell, winner of the 1982 Pony Marathon, had to drop out of the '83 race, a mile before the finish owing to dehydration.

One of the reasons he put it down to was the fact that in the Packhorse Hotel, Bolton, where the invited runners were accommodated, the bedroom tumblers were daintily small. You'd drunk a whole tumblerful of water, you thought, but it was less than the usual amount. Certainly we had been having a gorgeously hot spell of weather, and race day was no exception. But the body's need for fluid isn't satisfied just by drinking during the race. It's what has been drunk for several days beforehand that has an all-important effect. So, drink a little as often as possible, so that the body can absorb the fluid.

When Don is told, "You do look ill", he's pleased. "I know I must be fit", he told us. "We're the élite now; before, we were nutters."

Maximum VO_2 is needed to run a marathon and the higher the level, the better the runner. Your style affects your efficiency. To put heels down first is natural, but try to lengthen your stride. An extra inch added, cuts a mile off the marathon. That's worth thinking about. The more running you do, the muscles get shorter, so stretch continually and improve mobility. Strengthen leg muscles by step-ups and hill running. When running up, take shorter strides and use the arms in a pumping motion. Aim to get the heel outside the knee, and always get feet back to the ground fast. If hills aren't conveniently near, run wearing a tyre around your middle. Wearing heavy army-type boots is another way to improve your VO_2 through strength and resistance exercises. Whatever strengths and capacities you're born with, remember that they can be improved, with the exception of your maximum VO_2. That is controlled by your genes, VO_2 being the amount of oxygen your body is able to utilise from the air in your lungs.

The following letter was written from Africa:

Dear Ms Sharples,

I dictate this while sitting on a business-trip aeroplane to New York. I have just been reading your column in the January/February issue of *Running* magazine.

I remember last March, after the London Marathon, watching you on television. If I might say so, your splendid performance and example have been such an inspiration to me. I am still on the young side of 50, and I can amble around a marathon in about 2.40, so I feel there is still something of the "young dog" in my legs and lungs, not to say between my ears. But I do want to assure you how much you mean to so many people. I have heard people talk about you with wonder, in Nairobi, New York, San Francisco, and lots of other places in between. I am sure you have been told all this before, but here is another voice to suggest that your spirit – in your smile as much as in your muscles – helps many people down their own particular marathons of life, even if they never run a single step.

With best wishes to you – do keep on truckin'.

13 The New York Marathon

The *Running* Tour for the New York Marathon, 250 strong, met at Heathrow, under the leadership of Andy Etchells, the Editor. There was so much friendliness, I felt I knew the group before we even got on the plane.

A note from my diary – Thursday 22 October, 1981:

Concorde has just taken off as we sit here in our Aer Lingus plane, ready for our humbler ascent. An inspiration, diamond slim, thrusting upwards to the sky, and every one of the hearts on this plane has the same upward thrusting determination to finish that 26.2 miles in New York in as good a time as possible. A sparkling morning, and a swift trip to Woking station. Crowds of eager travellers lined up beside their cases.

"You're Madge", said a smiling Bob Iles, an AAA judge for field events from Portsmouth. "How's your training going?" We'd both had a hiatus after our last long runs of 20 miles, and so felt kin. Mine was caused by a knee pain that had come inexplicably as I turned a corner on the stairs at home, rushing to take a phone call, and a stiff neck that had come overnight.

"We want a photo at the foot of the plane steps", said a smiling Aer Lingus official, "and we want you at the front. Do you mind?" Of course I didn't, but was concerned in case the group would think me pushy, going to the front. T-shirts and flight bags were given out, handshakes and smiles all around. "May I have your autograph?" said the girl checking my luggage. "You're the most celebrated person on this Tour", said the girl in the queue behind me. There is such a bond between us, the bond of fear. But the well trained are confident and at ease. And the others, self included, are putting on a cool look.

A steward was waiting at the top of the steps: "I want to shake your hand. Welcome aboard and good luck". Later, I was taken to the pilots' cabin and, looking out through the cabin windows, gasped at the amazing breadth and beauty around us. "Is this what made you become pilots?" I asked them. "Actually, we'd never seen it when we decided to train". They told me of a fellow pilot who runs, and is so thin and fleshless, he can't sit comfortably for a seven hour flight without an air cushion. Sitting beside me were Paul Barrington King, who had run last year in 2.59.52, and Mike Fiori. They showed me this poem:

"If you think you're beaten, you are.
If you think you are not – you don't.
If you like to win but think you can't
It's almost certain you won't.
If you think you'll lose, you're lost
For oft in the world we find
Success begins with a fellow's will:
It's all in the state of your mind.
If you think you're outclassed you are:
You've got to think high to rise;
You've got to be sure of yourself
Before you can ever win a prize.
Life's battles don't always go
To the strongest or fastest man:
But soon or late, the man who wins
is the man who thinks he can!"

From *The Ghost Runner, John Tarrant's Own Story.*
Published by *Athletics Weekly.*

As we settled down to enjoy lunch, I listened to the chatter around me. "Finlandia marathon was tough." "Les, he's good on hills, once he gets his mileage, he'll do a good marathon." "I think the minimum is 60 miles per week; if you're below that, you're really pushing yourself." "Runs every lunchtime." "Goes over every day. Good track to train on, if it's not waterlogged."

New York seen from the air, was surprisingly green and suburban. But then, we weren't flying near the real city centre. We drove down to our hotel, the Milford Plaza, on 45th Street and 8th Avenue, a programme's throw from Broadway. It was crammed with runners come for the glamour marathon, French, German, South African, Norwegian, Australian and British.

In bed that night, trying to sleep, among the sirens of police cars and hooting of Medicare vans I noticed the clanging of a fire engine, then another and another. And they all seemed to stop below my bedroom window. I reached for the telephone, "The hotel is on fire, evacuate the hotel", said a voice.

Smoke and fumes were already in the corridor as I peeped out. On went my precious running shoes and a track suit over my nightie. Flight bag in hand, I rushed to the lifts and stairs. "We ought to go down the stairs", I said to a huddle of men. But the staircase was the source of the smoke and fumes. "Remember Towering Inferno", said one. We sniffed, remembered we were on the top floor of the Hotel, the 28th, and waited. How high do street ladders go? Firemen with long-handled axes came to assure us that the fire was now under control, and that we could go back to bed. The fire was on the 17th floor. We laughed afterwards when someone said it was just a warm up for the race.

Next day, we went along Broadway to register at the Sheraton Center, the race HQ. What a sight that was! Stalls of every known make of running gear, electrolyte drinks, vitamin-packed iced yoghurt. Just knowing that we were mingling with the cream of the world's marathon runners was intoxicating.

"Hallo, Madge. Great to see you, can I have a photo with you?" Greetings came from all sides. As I registered, Erika Tedder of Tadworth, Surrey, approached me. "I listened to you on 'Today' and 'Midweek' and started running to follow your example. My prize was to come to New York for the marathon, so I'm here because of you. How exciting to meet you."

Grete Waitz was seated at a table, and she normally waits for no-one, but I waited with delight for her to sign my running number 'Best Wishes to Madge Sharples from Grete Waitz'. That made it precious.

On Saturday, we gathered at 7.30 a.m. to run to the United Nations Plaza. That was a day to let the spirits soar. Blue skies over sparkling skyscrapers with automatically washed windows. Under the flags of 57 nations, 3,000 runners gathered to hear speeches of welcome from Fred Lebow, the organiser of the New York Marathon and the president of the American Amateur Athletic Association. Dr. Bill Pomeroy phoned me later. "I'm just going to South Africa, but I took a photo of you at the UN Plaza and I'd like to send it to you in England."

We ran an easy two miles to the Tavern on the Green, Central Park, for a fruit yoghurt and nutty bagels breakfast, laughing, talking, high on pressure and anticipation. I sat at a round table of New York cops, and Bill got a photo of that too. Back for our bus trip around the marathon route, organised by *Running*. Paul King gave us a first class commentary "Watch the corners here . . . that bridge will tire you . . . No, you can't get lost, there's a blue line painted in the middle of the road, all the way." As our tour concluded, away from Central Park, a hush of sadness fell as we drove past the Dakota Buildings entrance where John Lennon fell.

On to see the Metropolitan Opera House, more photographs, more handshakes. One crowded hour of glorious life. . . . Everyone here was having them all the time.

On to a super meal, generously provided by *The Runner*. Delicious wine, soft white bagels and jam. Then, back to the hotel, whacked out for pre-race preparations. I didn't dare go to the pasta party organised by the New York Road Runner's Club, thinking I ought to conserve what energies I had and get extra rest; but that night, a warm one too, the hotel switched on its central heating that made an intolerable noise. I couldn't turn it off, so I turned on the air conditioning as well and orchestrated the unwelcome noises.

Up at 3 a.m. raring to go. Ridiculous. Washed my hair. Wondered what the top runners were thinking, tossed uneasily and went down to breakfast at 6.45 a.m. Prunes, orange juice, bacon and scrambled egg. "So you're not running today, Madge." I edged off the bacon. Breakfast at the Milford Plaza was a delight. A help yourself buffet and then sitting at big round tables where we made friends. Voices were all around me. "Did 20 squats." "Ran 400 yards this morning." "How do you account for your success?" "Celibacy." "If my knee cracks up, I'll wait for you."

Soon we were off in our special bus. "I can see Salazar limping. I've got a chance. 25 mph limit! I'll need to slow down there." Excitement mounted as we reached Staten Island for the start.

Registration, visit to loo, queues ten deep, past the longest urinal in the world. Then a long wait on the road. I sat down, and all I could see was a forest of hairy legs, bristling with cold and excitement.

I was at the 4 hours 30 minutes plus board, among the fatties – no the cuddlies – and first-timers. Suddenly the cannon boomed and a

The New York Marathon

great wave of emotion went through us, a real physical sensation. All those hours of rain-running, the sweat-soaked clothes, the TV programmes we've missed, the winds we've battled against, and the hours of sleep we've lost – all to be justified now.

Tears welled up. "May I run beside you?" It was Erika.

The upward slope of the Verrazano Bridge is equal to 17 flights of stairs, I'm told. It was only as I ran down two miles later on the far side that I realised I'd never noticed we were going uphill. The views of distant ocean, beaches, ships, and eastwards, New York's skyline, plus the sight of all the eager excited faces was enough to lift mind and heart above all physical sensation. We were running on spirit alone. That lasted for about eight miles. Then I noticed I was comfortable.

On to the Pulaski Bridge – halfway – 2.17, my personal best. Bridges were the toughest part because the iron grids were hard on the feet. The Queensboro' Bridge was worse, and it had a soft carpet laid down to help us. (Rumour said they sold it off in foot squares as mementoes.) This bridge has a railway line running above it, held up by pillars. All along the bridge, runners were stretching out cramped muscles by holding on to these pillars. It was touching to see how many were being helped by other runners, massaging and warming their cramped legs.

Water and electrolyte drinks stops were every mile, and pieces of orange, chewing gum, sweets and lollipops were offered elsewhere by the crowd. I ate ten pieces of orange, and threw away the peel. So, if the 12,099 runners who finished before me, tossed away ten pieces of peel (and they might well have eaten more than ten) then I ran over 120,000 pieces of orange peel, a peril in itself.

The cheering crowds were massed at First Avenue: "Momma, Granma you can do it". "You're great, you're beautiful." I watched out for the 17 mile phone box at First Avenue and 76th Street where I was to record with Sue MacGregor for 'Woman's Hour'. While I supped honey she had brought me, with a silver spoon, she described how I was feeling with me joining in, and then said: "Now I'd like some photographs". "I suppose you'll want me to run back and then come forward?" "Yes." So off I went, knees aching now, but strange waves of energy coming when there were crowds shouting, and a slow drag across the bridges where there were none.

"I'm 72", said a man running beside me, "and I like to chat. Where you from? Winchester! that's part of London!" I couldn't go on letting him think that, so I explained about it being the ancient capital of England, when I thought, "This is crazy, I'm running a marathon, not giving a history lesson", and ran on ahead. He was pretty good at 72 to have breath to spare to chat, I hope he found someone else to talk to.

It was a perfect day for a marathon, 25 October, pearly-grey with a cool breeze. Afraid of getting chilled, I'd started in old slacks and a track suit jacket over my merino wool footless tights and yellow silk 'Ron Hill' shorts with a yellow Wessex Bodyscanner Appeal T-shirt under a blue running vest. All this was topped by a Union Jack dish-towel, contrived into a Robin Hood hat. When I had bought the towel, I told the shop assistant I wanted to wear it in the New York Marathon. "Come back tomorrow," she said, and there was the cleverly made hat ready for me. The slacks and jacket were thrown away early in the race, but the hat is still with me.

The going was tougher now, knees ached and body was tired, but the road surface was flat, past the shops and skyscrapers of First Avenue, to the Bronx. "Momma, Granma, you can make it." Running there was fantastic, the energy of the men and women, stamping on the ground, punching the air, shouting "This is for you, Momma", came across. I felt magically revitalised. My stride lengthened and I began to pass people.

As we entered Central Park, lots of runners had 'blown up' and were walking. I ran up the curving hill, passing people by the dozen. The strength in my legs seemed to come from all the shouts and cheers.

On and on, curving this way and that. "Madge, Madge, I've seen you on the TV in England. You're looking great, you're looking beautiful." "I cain't believe it, she's 65 and look at that stride! I just cain't believe it." The current of love that spreads along every marathon route is a really dynamic force.

I ran on, faster than I've ever run in my life, round, up and down, fingers tingling with pins and needles, and wondering if I was going to kill myself. But I wanted to beat five hours. Into the final straight, sweetest running of all, and the clock said 4.52.58. I could hardly believe it – 37 minutes off my personal best.

Off came my computer strip and I went into the funnel, where girls were standing chatting, but I was in such a hurry to get to the BBC studio in the Rockefeller Building on Fifth Avenue that I climbed out again, ran past them, then climbed in again to get my medal. And then I dissolved into a jelly-like state. A yellow oilskin-clad official supported me. "Will you help me get a taxi?" I asked anxiously.

"I can't, but he will", and I was literally handed on to someone else, and someone else, and then a firm English voice said: "Don't worry, I'll get you there", and Paul Kanssen of the London Marathon Organising Committee took charge. A huge foil blanket draped around me, a bottle of Perrier in my hand, and off we went, across Central Park, past camels and zebras in a zoo.

"Are you OK Madge?" Andy Etchells' voice was concerned. "I see you are". And he was gone, to welcome home others in the party. Now the happiness of a personal best and coming second in my age group, could tingle through me.

Everything seemed a long way away – or was it my wobbliness? – but we got there. I couldn't have managed without Paul's help. Medals and silver foil shimmered but the runners' happiness outshines anything material.

That evening, I watched the presentation of awards to the new world record holders Alberto Salazar and Alison Roe, with John and Sylvia Disley. We were joined by Chris Brasher and my heroine Leslie Watson, who took me to join her party for dinner. Chris and Leslie were both presented with awards, Chris receiving a gold medal and Leslie a silver dish.

Next morning's breakfast lasted over two hours, while I listened to everyone's 'Marathon Story'. But that was the delight of being in a group tour. That day, I had to go to four banks, and wait in a queue in each one, before one would accept Barclay's Bank dollar travellers' cheques – and they would only exchange $100. The bank's counter reached my chin. I laid my head on it and almost wept with weariness and frustration. New Yorkers seemed resigned to queues in banks and hotel check-outs. But most would be like me, temporary residents.

Tuesday's highlight was lunch at the Peking Restaurant with Taiko Sakami, President of the New York Branch of the American Association of University Women, and Margaret Blemker, its secretary. After our Peking Duck and Tofu, which were delicious, Margaret took me on a wonderful tour of central New York; in to St. Patrick's Cathedral and other churches, with stories about each one. How one was incorporated in a skyscraper, so that the church remained as a church, and benefited from the sale of the land. That one is much used by young people for pop concerts.

We went on to 'The Market' where I admired the relaxed yet cultured atmosphere of book shops, plants and trees, and pretty places to sit and eat. Frozen yoghurt was popular.

Wednesday's treat was a matinée of 'Forty-Second Street' on Broadway. Bob Iles and I paid $25 each to stand at the back of a gallery, but it was a great show. As the band struck up, I was seized by uncontrollable sobbing, so many teen-age memories were linked to the music. I had to get down on the floor to hide my tears. Back to the Milford Plaza to change, and off to a party for us 103 marathoners, organised by *Running* at 'The English Pub', Broadway. Spare ribs, meat balls, pasta and anything we wanted to drink. I could hardly get on with eating, so many wanted a photograph of themselves with me.

"Silence for a speech from the runner who had best 'personal best' of us all." So I had to say a few words and tell everyone about the Winchester marathon coming up in the spring. To my delight, 60 people asked for application forms.

After that, a trip to the top of the Empire State Building with Bob seemed the most natural thing to do. It was midnight as we walked down 42nd Street! It didn't seem any different from the other streets in that neighbourhood.

14 Sports Review of 1981

It was wildly exciting. A letter from Harold Anderson of BBC TV inviting me to be present at the Sports Review of 1981, when the Sports Personality of the Year would be announced. I rang up the Kensington offices to ask anxiously, "What should I wear?" "A short evening dress", was the answer. I really ought to have known, there's no such thing in the sartorial calendar. However, having decided that I'd wear white and gold, I found an evening dress that wasn't quite full length – white silk draped harem trousers with a top of gold sequins. A boob tube was more exposed than I'd have liked, but it was white and gold, and there wasn't much choice in Winchester. We were to be put up at the Kensington Hilton, have a buffet dinner at the TV centre, and go on the air at 8 p.m.

I arrived at the Hilton about 5 p.m. to enjoy the luxury of a private bath and a pot of tea. By this time, my mascara had run, and the professional make-up that I'd had that morning was a little the worse for wear. The hotel shop stocked Yardley's make-up, so I was able to repair the damage. Into the boob tube, rather tight for me, gold sandals and Chinese mink coat that I'd really have liked to keep on, and out into London's glittering lights. Snow was underfoot and rain falling, but 9 December is far enough away from Christmas for shop displays to be sparkling. I felt sparkling too.

The TV cameras were waiting as I left my taxi. The BBC TV Centre is a huge circle of garden space, with circular buildings rising behind. I looked around for a door, but in the glare of the lights, couldn't see one, but saw the camera following me, and just walked forward into darkness. All in best Hollywood style. It was fun, anyway, even if never to see the light of a TV set. A charming girl, Julia, took me upstairs to a cloakroom and buffet reception. I was a little nervous about leaving my mink; probably there were so many better ones that I needn't have worried.

With a gin and tonic, I went round the wheelchaired guests who were disabled. How can we ever feel smug about what we've done, when they're fighting against their infirmities before they even start the sports. It was moving to be with them, and hear of their prowess from Ken Black of the National Star Centre who invited me down to see their Cheltenham College. After a chicken and salad meal with a delightful young man in evening dress, with a frilled shirtfront – I felt at home with him. "It's all I've got with me", he said, "I've just got back from an exhibition match at Cowdenbeath." That should have given me the clue about who he was, but I didn't realise until next day, the World Champion of Snooker, Steve Davis. Also a World Champion of Charm.

As more and more celebrities arrived, I got out my camera and had photos taken. Perhaps it was a form of conceit, but I didn't want photos of other people, I just wanted photos of celebrities with me. Frank Bough, who got a bit impatient as I explained the workings of my camera to whoever was acting as cameraman, Ardiles and Villa who wrote a charming message in Spanish on my invitation card; Ron Hill, Steve Davis, Tony Gubba, who presented the TV outdoor broadcasts of the first two London marathons so admirably and some, that in my abysmal ignorance of sporting celebrities, I didn't recognise. Celebrities like Seb Coe and Bob Champion went straight to their seats in the auditorium.

It was like a circus tent, steeply pitched rows on either side of an oval, audience on one side, celebrities on the other. I was in the third front row, beside Bob Wiseman (aged 78) immaculately spruce, silver haired and erect, the oldest man in the London Marathon. Wired for sound, the clips attached to my boob tube, I wondered was mine the high wire act or the trapeze. Both sides of the oval were 'high' in anticipation of the programme to come, and while cameras, lights and readers were wheeled into place, and a multitude of wires arranged, we were shown a film of 'Mistakes of '81', a rollicking farce.

"Now we're into the final straight", and a racing car would ricochet off film in a cloud of dust. "And the winner of the race is . . ." – total blackout. The story of filming was epitomised for me, when 'Nationwide' were videoing me with Desmond Lynam (before I went to New York) by the taut, white knuckles of Derek Mitchell, the producer. And the end product was only me.

To a first time onlooker, getting this show on the road was a fantastic feat of organisation, adaptability and team work. When the satellite picture of Sue Barker didn't come through, and the whole programme moved 15 minutes forward, hopefully waiting for Sue, all went on as if every move had been planned. But that was improvisation. There was no sign but that everything was going according to schedule, perfectly. I take my hat off to the commentators, Harry Carpenter and Frank Bough, and their colleagues moving equipment here and there. There was a circus atmosphere: clowns were about to jump through paper hoops; and tigers were going to be brought on.... Roger Moodie of BBC TV had led me to my seat, and as we passed through the crowds, "Whoever's sitting beside Madge will have some fun".

There we were, hushed expectancy one moment, babble of conversation the next "I'm going to ask you questions", said Frank Bough, "but I won't tell you what they are, because I know whatever I say you'll come up with something." Steve Davis was below me, and Wallie the blind runner with his guide. The Sports Personality of the Year Award was won by Ian Botham, and we saw him, in India, being presented with a replica of the award, a stainless steel BBC camera mounted on wood. Seb Coe, Bob Champion and Steve Davis won awards too. I was so glad Wallie was given a trophy (stainless steel BBC camera) though I felt it should have been a joint trophy, shared with his guide, who smilingly led him here and there.

Cricket, cricket, racing and more cricket, and then Frank was asking Bob Wiseman how long he was going to run. Bob expects to peak when he's 80. Marvellous. My turn, and I don't quite remember exactly what I said. I do know I forgot to hold shoulders back and bosom up. But I do remember the great roar of laughter coming from the audience when I said that the last race I ran in, was for the under tens on a Sunday school trip. And I didn't even win that. Frank asked me how I felt about running through the streets of London in tiny satin shorts, at my age. And on Sunday too! By the tone of his voice I could sense that he expected me to feel awkward about it. But when you're running a marathon, it's how comfortable and suitable for the weather your clothes are, that's on your mind, much more than their propriety. Though Joyce Smith has said that she never goes running without her mascara and Leslie Watson her perfume, I use lipstick, though it soon must get washed off.

Frank asked me what made me run. I was just meandering into the beauties of nature, hares boxing in March, pheasant cocks fighting in the January snows, a ritual ballet dance of such grace and beauty that has held me in thrall to cross-country running ever since, when Frank cut me short. Professionalism was brought home to me.

After the show, we went to the reception. I won't say all hell was let loose, but about ten times as many people than had been on stage were there. Again, there was cold chicken, sandwiches of salad, mince pies, and every kind of drink. Row upon row of non-alcoholic bottles standing at the ready, and waitresses going round with the stronger stuff. I stuck to white wine from start to finish, some sweeter, some *pétillant*, all delicious. I'd hoped to meet, or even see Jimmy Savile, Seb Coe or Sir Douglas Bader, but though I struggled through the crowds from one reception area to another, up and down crowded staircases, I didn't see any of them.

Autograph hunting was impossible in the crush. Lots of men came and congratulated me, I don't quite know what for, but it was all very gratifying and heart warming. Gnawed more chicken, drank more kinds of wine, chatted to innumerable men, who they were, I haven't any idea, and I can't say they looked sporty, but they all knew me. At last I was waiting for a taxi, with world record holding swimmers and we all went back to the International Hilton. Off with the make-up and into bed. 1.45 a.m.

My phone rang at 8.30 a.m. No-one answered to tell me why, so I got up fast, ignoring the longing for a shower or bubble bath, or morning tea and went down to breakfast. A cheerful little curly, red-headed girl joined me, and we chose fruit juice and fruit and sat together. Amazingly, she was the Judo World Champion. Soon we were joined by the Olympic Silver Medal rower. Her hair shone and she was lovely. Both impressed me so much that I realised now was the time to collect autographs. So, taking the red rose decorated breakfast mats, that the two ladies had used I went round.

"You were at last night's show?" I asked a burly looking man, passing my table – at least a Rugby International. "No, I wasn't. Actually, I'm in antiques." Just then, Bob Wiseman joined me and we had a good laugh. Soon, a sweet, delicate looking and so charming lady drank coffee with us, the lady Snooker World Champion. She lectures at the Northumberland College of Education where I did teacher training back in 1967–8. A disused factory in my day, with rough wood partitions and staircases, that is now bulldozed to the ground, and a fine new polytechnic has taken its place.We chatted about colleagues and teachers I'd known, while I collected autographs on the place mats from as many athletes as I could spot.

After my extended breakfast, Gillian Harland of *Annabel* came along to interview me in the lounge over orange juice and smoked salmon sandwiches. "You've given me a life story", she said. "I'll send you a proof of what I select and you'll sign it before it's printed." That sounds, and is, very reasonable. But the way some of the things were phrased, or accented, I didn't like and would have altered. But that meant altering much more that I did like, in order not to spoil the style of the article. In the end, I left it as it was. Now, I realise it is the writer's job to be worrying about style. I should just have slashed out what I didn't want.

After my interview, packing up and meeting hotel staff who were interested in running, and our forthcoming Winchester marathon in particular, I was glad to sit down in the lounge again for tea. How very English it looked. Chocolate brown heavy stoneware pot and curved heat-preserving cups. But I didn't get drinking mine hot. "May I congratulate you", an athletic-looking man came across, "you were great, I saw the programme last night." "And you're an athlete?" I asked him. "Yes, a professional footballer for 15 years. I still keep up some of the training, enough to keep fit." We chatted. More tea. More congratulations. More tea.

So I came out to slushy streets and Christmas lights. I was taking a bus to Adam's home in south London, when a woman carrying a crying baby got on. "Full up, off", said the conductor. "God love you," she replied, stepping into the falling snow. Then the passengers began to talk. "How could he?" from one side. "If there was an accident he'd be in trouble and lose his job", from the other. If we'd been sincere, I felt, one of us should have got off the bus to let the woman stay, before we criticized the conductor. But we all had such good reasons to stay on. "Got to be at work ." "Got to catch a train."

I was going to be within the bosom of my family. (But, burdened with luggage I still could have got off.) "Sometimes", I told Adam, "I just ache to be with you all." That's Everymother speaking. I like to see the gifts I've brought back from abroad: the blue Bolivian woven handbag; the fascinating tasselled and textured Tibetan wall-hanging from Kathmandu; onyx from Argentina; amethyst from Brazil.

Around this time, I went to a Ramblers Holidays Leaders' conference. On the way home I wrote: "Everyone has a good book in him. Yet, how many people do we know who have had books published? Look around. How do they spend their free time? Have they any free time to spend?"

Every one of the 209 delegates at the conference was a Leader, ready at all times to hold forth to two people or 200, without the slightest hesitation. Can you imagine the noise level in the dining room and in the bars? We are passing Woking, and I see an advert for the Yvonne Arnaud theatre 'Two and Two Make Six'. How trivial that seems, when our minds have been on Delphos, African wildlife and Kilimanjaro, mystic prayer flags flapping cold and lonely in Nepal, seen by only whom?

The following articleappeared in the *Winchester Extra* on 7 January, 1982:

The Winning that was 1981

In the last year, the name Madge Sharples has become synonymous with marathon running. The fact that her urge to join the craze for pounding world-wide cities' streets at retiring age has only made her more of a personality. Women's programmes have hounded her, television sporting programmes have polished up new pedestals and marathon followers the world over have wrung her hands, bent her ears and lavished her with gifts and compliments. She doesn't spend so much time at home in Winchester's Andover Road these days.

The tiny Scots voice takes on the wonder of a child when she says: "What a fantastic year it's been".

"It's been an adventure in communication. Running is almost a religion, cutting across colour, creed and class. It has brought me so much, and I hope it has for others."

This time last year, the University trained brain was content to tramp various parts of the world writing on flora and fauna between spells at her civil servant's desk at Worthy Down's RAPC Depot, and keeping fit with a bit of jogging.

Since then she has been halfway round the world in a mass of starts including the recently introduced London Marathon.

But probably her happiest memories are of America and the various events to evolve out of the year's 'daddy of them', the New York Marathon.

Now, while planning a running programme to exhaust a centipede in 1982, Madge looks back on the running, the feting and the recognition she won States-side.

She spoke to many gatherings on her life, gave interviews over mammoth breakfasts and wondered at the comparatively lavish life-style of the American working-class.

But the gruelling 26 miles 385 yards she pounded out of New York's streets made more than just an impact on her feet!

By kind permission of the *Basingstoke Gazette*.

15 'Sport for All' launch

The Scottish Health Council had invited me to be present at the launching of the 1982 'Sport for All' programme, the special theme being 'Women in Sport'. It was held at a very fine sports centre at Giffnock, Glasgow, on 20 January. Linsey Macdonald made an excellent opening speech, and Dee Hepburn and I ran here and there with her for the benefit of the dozens of photographers. They were lovely young girls, as friendly and unspoilt as they were bonny. The following article appeared in the *Daily Express* on 21 January, 1981:

On Your Marks Girls, and Get Set to Run from the Kitchen Sink.

MADGE SHARPLES always wanted to stand on the slopes of Everest. But she didn't leave it as another kitchen sink daydream – she got on her mark, got set, and did it.

Madge was 62, but that didn't bother her. She started a series of daily runs to get fit. Today, three years later, she has fulfilled her dream of seeing the highest mountain in the world. *And* she has run in the New York and London marathons.

Very soon after I started running I realised I loved it", said Glasgow born Madge. "The last time I ran in a race I was a nine-years-old schoolgirl."

She was a guest of the Scottish Sports Council yesterday at the launch of their Sport For All 1982 campaign. This year the theme is Women and Sport. Madge, a mother of four, said: "I think this campaign is a great idea. Any woman can take up some kind of sport.

Medallist

"I have also enjoyed coming here and meeting Scottish sports-women of all ages who love their sport."

The star guest at the lunch in Eastwood recreation centre near Glasgow, was elfin Olympic bronze medallist runner Linsey Macdonald, 17. But if you could pick a woman to give heart to the 14 out of 15 women in Scotland who do not regularly take part in sport, Madge would be the one.

For those who are no longer sweet 17, Madge is closer to reality. She is proof that sport is enjoyable and good for your face and figure – even in later life. Slim, bright-eyed and attractive, she oozes good health. She regularly jogs ten miles a day – at 65, remember – and recommends it to anyone.

Madge and Linsey were accompanied by former Olympic swimmer Cissy Hunt and tennis player Joyce Hulme.

Even Scotland's best known lady footballer was there – East Kilbride actress Dee Hepburn, who played a footballer in the much acclaimed Scottish film 'Gregory's Girl'.

"I have always enjoyed swimming and sport and this undoubtably helped me keep fit during the four weeks of football training, I had to go through before filming started," she said.

"But I would certainly recommend more women to take up sports." Linsey goes through a gruelling training programme as a matter of course, yet she still finds it fun. "People are often put off training outdoors because of cold wet weather," she said.

"But it's not as tough as it looks and you don't have to be competing at international level to enjoy it."

The girls were accompanied by the campaign mascot, Donna.

By kind permission of the *Daily Express*.

Both the BBC and Independent Scottish TV showed their interviews of us that evening, and Radio Clyde put out an interview with me next morning. It was a very happy occasion, especially for me, to be back again with 'ma, ain folk'. I was staying with a nephew, David Pope, his wife Anne and their four lovely young children Stephen, Lesley, Douglas and Euan. Each evening I would go out to run in the dark, for there wasn't time during the daylight hours. I'd run for a couple of hours, out by Rouken Glen, and was always rather pleased with myself when I arrived back at the time intended, as I was running purely by my 'bump of location' and didn't bother with a map, which would require glasses to be of any use.

When I knocked at a front door one evening, to ask for a glass of water, a lady signalled through the glass door that she couldn't open to me. Perhaps she was afraid I was a decoy. I wonder what treasures she was protecting? Perhaps she just had a sore foot! While at the BBC TV studios at Queen Margaret Drive (to discuss a February programme with producer Elizabeth Halliday) word reached me that the Lord Provost of Glasgow, Dr. Michael Kelly, would like to meet me that afternoon. Lunch at the BBC – herrings in oatmeal, couldn't be more appropriate – and off in a taxi to fulfil a dream.

I'd gazed in awe as a child at the marbled magnificence, Renaissance mosaics and elaborate carvings of Glasgow's City Chambers. Now, I wasn't just entering them, I was invited to that holy of holies, the Lord Provost's Apartment. The huge room had windows on two sides, and was bright with sunshine and a blazing fire. Dr. Michael Kelly was taking off his jacket as I went in, and plunged right into a subject close to his heart: "How much training would I need to do, to run a marathon?" "Can you give about two hours a day?" I asked, and his face fell. There was no way he could do that. I wish I'd said less, to give him hope. After all, just because I needed that amount of time, he might have needed less. We went on to discuss fitness generally, and he told me of his plans to hold an autumn marathon in Glasgow. He was so friendly and approachable that I went on to tell him another of my childhood wishes – to write for the *Glasgow Herald*.

He phoned at once and made an appointment for me to meet the sports editor and Anne Simpson, women's editor. I went home with a commission – to write a monthly column of about 700 words giving advice about getting fit for the Glasgow Marathon. I was already writing a similar page for *Running*, and a weekly one for the *Southampton Advertiser*. No Problem. I got to work right away:

Marathons Bring a Touch of Magic

Marathons bring a touch of magic to a city. There's a flow of emotion that links runners and spectators, expressing the singleness of purpose that is going to get those pounding feet over 26.2 miles of hard road. That's where the magic stops. They say that a runner is someone who slumps into the nearest armchair, exhausted through continual training and coping with life's 101 duties. But she's content and fulfilled, revelling in the satisfaction of rest after exercise, a wonderful feeling.

The London Gillette Marathon, March 1981, was my first marathon, my previous racing experience having been one for the under tens, at a Sunday School trip. But I've walked (and worked) hard all my life and had a go at the usual sports, over the years, golf, tennis, squash, badminton, ski-ing, dancing and swimming, and gardening too. Perhaps bringing up four children in 17 homes in 22 years in England and South America was good stamina training and we did live at 12,000 feet up in Andes, in Bolivia.

"Why do you go on running?" I'm often asked. "Because I love running, meeting people and exploring fresh experiences." My next is flying to Bermuda to run in my fifth marathon since March, 1981. About a thousand international marathoners are expected to take part. Bermuda, whose speed limit is 20 mph (that won't worry me) is a string of 138 islands, linked by causeways and bridges, no more than two miles wide, offering a beautiful route on different shores, with 'interesting' hills. Coves of pink sand, below the crystal clear waters of the Atlantic will be a welcome haven afterwards.

Running is such a simple sport, any time, anywhere, any length, and any weather, alone or with others. We've formed the Wessex Joggers here at Winchester, and run on Sunday mornings, 3, 7 and 13 miles in small groups. A car goes behind us, with a big notice 'Warning – Runners Ahead', and another meets us at our halfway point, with drinking water. It's most important to drink before you start, and ideally, every two or three miles. If your body drew fluid from your blood, a strain would be put on the heart. In Glasgow, you are fortunate in having so many parks, and broad tar macadam pavements. I've enjoyed my evening runs in the Giffnock area, up, down and round about the good solid houses in quiet roads.

We hear about a 'Runner's High'. This can come, after 10 or 12 miles when, muscles in tune, running seems as natural as breathing, and a euphoric joy takes over. It's great to be alive; life sparkles. But, for that to come, you must be comfortable. Running shoes are one of the best investments you'll ever make, for they are scientifically designed to cushion the jarring, inevitable with road running, keep you cool, and give some measure of heel protection.

The injuries that could befall you are legion, as you'll learn, but with care, luck and a sensible, go-gradually training programme, they can be avoided. Learn to make use of every odd moment, to exercise. And the most important one is to stretch, stretch and stretch again. Stretch in bed, thrusting out your heels, hard, toes pointing ceilingwards. Push knees with as much force as you can muster, hard against the sheets. When you get up, circle shoulders, forwards and backwards, then 'punch' the ceiling, arms stretched out above your head. Get up on tip toes too, and punch hard. Now, imagine you have a paintbrush held in both hands, and 'paint' the biggest circle in the world. At least , if you're stretching as hard as you can, that's how it will feel. Start training by running on the spot, near an open window. I began by doing 'Knees up Mother Brown' in the back garden, while preparing breakfast. When I was out of breath, the eggs were done to a turn. When you're confident, jog to a park, or where there's little traffic, and do what the crowds shouted to me in the New York Marathon: "Momma, Momma, let yourself go!"

Working at Worthy Down, the Royal Army Pay Corps camp, five miles out of Winchester, I was lucky that I could run to the office, cross country, or by road. That took about an hour, each way, and I ran at lunch times as well, or gave my colleagues a yoga lesson. Yes, two-and-a-half hours minimum each working day. LSD (Long Slow Distance) came at weekends for, once I'd been accepted for the London Marathon last March, training became an ethical matter, since over 12,000 were rejected. To be fair, I had to try as hard as I could. And I've gone on trying, and enjoying it, ever since; apprehensive before each marathon – oh, if I can only finish – ecstatically happy when I do. And you will be, too.

Build up to M-Day

Stretching exercises. Every muscle should be stretched every day. Running on the spot. Start training by walking and running one mile daily, gradually eliminating the walking. Slowly increase this until you can run:

Sunday – Four miles, long slow distance.
Monday – Rest.
Tuesday – Two miles, altering your pace, now fast, now slow.
Wednesday – Rest.
Thursday – Two or three miles, again altering your pace, or trying a hillier route.
Friday – Rest.
Saturday – Time yourself, starting with a one mile run.

Keep a log book of your runs, wear clothing that isn't tight or restricting, and don't miss any opportunities. Run to the shops, or to work. Several short runs in the day, will do you more good than one long one. Ideally, you should not run until two hours after a meal, but that can make problems. Better to run not too fast, after a light meal than not run at all. For three years, I enjoyed my porridge, two boiled eggs, toast and tea, and ran to work without ill effects. We all have to suit our way of life. Swimming is good on rest days.

By kind permission of the *Glasgow Herald*.

16 Bermuda

Bermuda's International marathon makes the perfect winter break for us Britons. It is run at the end of January. Even the morning plane journey is timed to be as comfortable as possible.

My diary says:

Airport lounge for Bermuda. Clothes worn around me, expensively casual, muted colours, baggy pants. Very few older people, some French, wearing inconsequential straw hats.

It is surprising to be recognised and greeted by airline staff – luggage checkers, ticket checkers and everyone, with a smile. Glad I remembered to get some gin before I left. We waited for flight time in the lounge and were called to our seats by numbered groups, very civilised, no standing or waiting. On board, tango music and softly-shaded lights. The middle seats are slightly staggered, so that my seat has open space in front and I can do my knee exercises. French in front: "Chess? Mais oui". Italians behind, and refined English voices on all sides.

I hope I can leave bucket shops alone in future. It was disconcerting to be told this morning that my homeward flight will arrive at 10.20 a.m. instead of 6.45 a.m. Arranging things by phone misses out details like that. Perhaps I could have got a timetable from somewhere and checked times myself. Had to phone Adam to say I probably won't make it to his wedding but will try. We are to lunch at Robert Carrier's, so I'll go straight there, if need be.

Smooth flight at 31,000 feet – seven hours. We're 100 miles off Cork, and gin and tonic in hand, I can look around. It's the most popular drink for the older folk. Orange juice or coke for the young, of whom there are a surprising number. How do they do it? Hurry on with the lunch and a siesta, this is absolute luxury, to be flying to Bermuda.

I'm thinking of my work, now distanced by four months of retirement. How did it arrive on my desk? That chokingly boring work, but who passed it to me, and under what rigorous checks? I can't remember. I'm free. My face is relaxing as I write the word 'free' the best word in the English language. No, it is 'love', but then, love can be one-sided and that brings so much pain. Have changed my seat – three empty ones beside me. Why did my legs hurt so much when I stood up and is that a passing sniffle or a cold? I'm shivering. Oh well, down with the gin.

Everyone around me seems to be chattering and laughing, irritatingly hyena-like. It's a relief to be alone, silent. They're taking orders for wines with lunch. I think I'll be an alcoholic. All I really want is to go to sleep after some food. Will I actually be swimming this p.m. and having a super dinner in the Bermudiana Hotel. Can hardly believe it. And all because I went on running and keeping fit – wind and weather not withstanding.

Some are reading thick books as if their lives depended on it. As if they've been waiting for this opportunity to read. Perhaps they have. Some are getting quite matey; a stout grey-haired lady is now leaning over the seat in front, to chat to the bald grey-headed occupant.

It's been quite an effort, just getting away. Everyone says, "Bermuda, how lovely, want someone to carry your bags?" But there's a bit of spade work behind it, more than just the running and training. First, I had to be sure of accommodation and do a bit of asking and reminding. Didn't do the latter soon enough, so lost the chance of an Apex flight. Rang round 'Adverts' in the *Guardian, Telegraph, Observer* and chose the cheapest. £10 more than Apex, but I could return, not in 14 days, but when I wanted. So far so good, but I didn't really trust the firm. And when, after I'd sent the £275 asked for, I phoned, and was asked to hold on, and was left hanging, not once, but three times, I wondered was this travel agency anything but a collector of cheques. In the end, I rang British Airways seat reservations and was reassured that my flight was booked.

When I arrived at Heathrow, all ready to fly, I was less assured when I was directed to the ticket payments desk. But all was well in the end, and I bore off my ticket thinking, "Never again make flight reservations with a bucket shop by phone." Perhaps it's all right if you can hand the money over a counter and receive your ticket on the spot, but I'd like to try that with a not too expensive fare. No doubt, one day, I'll find myself paying for a round-the-world-trip, in the cheapest possible agency, and then suffer the pangs of doubt, as to whether the agency is on the level.

After lunch, I went forward to meet the crew, Captain J. M. Daulby, FO John Lindsay and SEO Peter O'Brien. The sea glittered below us, it was a perfect flight. Word came to me that the High Sheriff of Lincolnshire would like to meet me, so I was taken to join him in the first class. He was charming, David Morrell, making a trip round the world, visiting members of his family *en route*. His first stop was Bermuda where, in the peace and quiet he hoped to find time (while staying with a friend) to finish the writing of a book.

I noticed, as we went through customs, he was having a little bother with his luggage, a huge suitcase that was being charged as excess. I guessed it contained the research papers for his book, and imagined his mounting bill for excess luggage as he continued his journey.

The airport at Bermuda is situated on the sea. As you step outside to get a taxi, hibiscus blossoms and pink oleanders fringe the waves lapping on the shore. It was the end of January, and the afternoon sun was warm in a light breeze.

My diary noted next morning:

> 7.30 a.m. Sunrise glow on the horizon; water rippling between the moored yachts and a strange bird is calling. Last night in the half dark, thought I saw an egret. Bermuda is amazing. Little volcanic islands, popping up from the sea, joined by bridges or causeways. This makes driving so attractive, for the sea is literally only a stone's throw away, most of the time.

On arrival, several of the plane's passengers recognised me and were wishing me well as we queued for luggage examination. "Souvenirs, gifts, liquor?" intoned the customs officer, which made me smile as I hadn't set foot outside the airport; but of course I might have been returning from anywhere. On the hour drive to my hotel (the Bermudiana, where THF have kindly invited me to stay, at a reduced rate) groups of children were going home from school dressed in very smart English-style uniforms. But I only saw one white child.

"How much are houses here?" I asked my driver. "100,000 dollars for five rooms and that wouldn't be near a road or the sea." "You pay hundreds of thousands for that. Very expensive." So were taxi fares. The houses all have steepish white painted roofs, even gate posts and public lavatories, so that rain can run down into inner tanks and be saved. Collection is a top priority. More birds calling now, traffic beginning.

The hotel is lovely – pink, all rooms balconied, overlooking the sea. My fourth floor balcony is roomsized. Last night, after dinner, I sipped a G & T, watching the sunset. Yachts, dinghies, boats of all sizes are strung out along the coastline, which is part of a big 'inland sea' protected by rock from the Atlantic. This gives protection and makes the islands such a heavenly place to live. Houses are dotted everywhere, roofs appearing among the trees. Tiny bays of pink sand and rocky headlands make dream hideaways. One district is even given the postal address of 'Fairy Land', and it is.

An article in the *Telegraph* reports that the Bermuda Information Office in London is objecting to paying collection costs of £300 for its daily two sacks of mail. Continuing interest in Bermuda. And I'm not surprised.

Last night at dinner, the wine waiter said, "You're tough, coming in light clothes", I noticed ladies were wearing tweed suits and woollies. Not 'dressed for dinner' at all; rather disappointing. After all I've read about Bermuda, I expected that pretty thin clothes and dressing-up would be the order of the day. But no, by the evening hours, from about 4 p.m. onwards, the air chills down. I felt it last night when I went over to the Elbow Beach Hotel, on South Shore, where the marathon HQ is centred, and where there are get-togethers and talks each evening. Dr. George Sheehan spoke last night, and actually recommended sugar; sweetness before and sweetness during running. He quoted an athlete who filled his tea with sugar until no more would dissolve, then drank it. "Take your sweetness in the morning, that's when the liver stores its glycogen," he said.

At breakfast a business man at the next table was joined by a colleague, "When I was in the Eighth Grade, I broke 100; 5ft 7in., in the Seventh Grade, 5ft 9in., in the Eighth". "I was 5ft 11in., in the Tenth Grade," countered his friend, "and I broke 100 then". They were men in their early forties, and I was amazed that they'd remembered the facts so accurately and discussed them, almost as an excuse for not running in the pre-marathon 10km. that day.

I went up to the stadium to watch; strong gusts of wind, hot sunshine and crowds of gaily dressed people, many in running outfits as I was; whether they were running or not. Before long, the runners were back with us, watching the back markers come in. Winner was Geoff Smith, in 28.14, at the head of the 30 runners to break the 30-minute mark. Grete Waitz finished 36th overall, first woman in 31.41, a course record, and her third win in so many years. I felt that I'd better make sure of finishing the marathon, by not tiring myself with flying out on the Friday, and running on the Saturday. It might have been too much of a good thing.

But I was keen to go on the marathon route tour, and we left the stadium in crowded buses at 1 p.m. Round the streets of Hamilton and along Front Street, then heading southwards, close to the sea. Our first stop was a supermarket, where most people seemed to be buying beer and fruit drinks. I was excited, nervous and apprehensive at the thought of that endless 26 miles next day, but determined to miss nothing.

Some 10km. race runners had joined us on the bus. "Oh, I passed you, you were hanging on that tree." "I fell down later on." They laughed. "It was only a coupla days ago, it's still sore." "The secret of running is to talk to your ancestors as you run." "When you start hopping around, you're not going to reach your potential." "About ten miles, it starts hurtin' bad. At 20, it's all I'm thinkin' about."

There were little booths at intervals along the road. "Anything that doesn't move, they'll sell." Everyone seemed to be wearing well-worn running shoes, all sorts of makes and colours of anoraks and track suits. Lines of bunting and flags were being put up for next day. But the sunshine, sparkling sea, pink sand and flowering bushes were more than enough to induce gaiety in the most overtrained and wearied runner. Score Palms, Pacific Island Euphorbia, Buttonwood,

Lavender cotton, Silverthatch, Pentecost Palms and Chinese Goddess Bamboos were there to delight.

Charles Gaylord was giving a party that evening, over Knapton Hill, at his home at 'The Hambletts', and I was delighted to be invited to join the company, almost all runners, who had gathered in the cedar-beamed house. Such delicious food, delicately prepared with no effort spared to make the presentation as colourful and tempting as possible. Carrot cake sounds so pedestrian, but it was a gastronomic triumph, the outer covering a shell for vegetarian delicacies underneath.

Wines flowed and so did talk, outside on moonlit verandahs, or lapped in comfort on huge sofas. No, we didn't stand around much. I treasure photographs of me taken with such celebrities as John Graham and Dr. George Sheehan. With a group I was back at the Bermudiana soon after 10 p.m. More than I were nervous about what lay ahead.

"Race day," says my diary, "up at 4 a.m. darkness and lights flashing on the water by moored boats. Slept fitfully until up at 7 a.m."

There wasn't an early runners' breakfast, so I went down at 8 a.m. and ate too much: cereal, orange juice, scrambled eggs and coffee. (The moment you sit down at a table, coffee is rushed to you. Then when I want it, it's either cold, or there's no one around to bring fresh.) I listened to other runners' talk. "There are 50 million Chinese who don't know this race is being run; it's not that important." "I'm not fast and I'm not slow, and I'm not a celebrity, I run for fun and it is absolute hell." "I'm a sixth generation New Yorker, and there's insanity in the family."

Up to the stadium and the start, by taxi; Well, it involved several hills, and I didn't want to get lost. Having a stadium start and finish certainly makes for runners' comfort. There's the last minute thinking, "Have I got tissues, are my shoe laces right, not too tight, not too loose. Ought I to wear a cotton T-shirt as well as a silky low necked running top? More sunburn cream? More lip cream to keep them soft? Is there time to go yet again to the toilet?" And I ran down to the start on the main road.

Here are the extensive pre-race medical instructions:

Medical Instructions for Runners

Temperature and Humidity
Temperature and humidity can substantially affect the performance and safety of runners. When the temperature exceeds 70°F (21°C) and/or humidity is greater than 50 per cent, the incidence of heat-related injury markedly increases. The race medical team will monitor these conditions and post coloured flags at the starting line to alert runners to the weather situation.

Flag Colour Condition
RED – Temperature is over 75°F or humidity is over 50 per cent. Runners who are sensitive to heat or humidity should carefully consider participation.
YELLOW – Temperature is over 70°F or humidity is over 45 per cent. Since both are likely to rise during the race, runners should be able to recognize significant changes in physical status. (See below).
GREEN – Temperature is below 70°F and humidity is below 45 per cent.

Recognition of Physical Problems
While every runner will experience varying degrees of discomfort, significant changes in physical status should be recognized. If in doubt, stop to ask for advice. Medical personnel, identifiable by red caps, will be positioned at all aid stations.
1 Symptoms of over-exertion: nausea, vomiting, extreme breathlessness, dizziness, unusual fatigue, headache.
2 Symptoms of heat injury: pilo-erection (hair on end or gooseflesh) on the chest or upper arms, chilling, headache or throbbing pressure, unsteadiness, vomiting or nausea, laboured breathing, faintness, muscle cramps. Continuing the race with these symptoms may result in collapse or unconsciousness. Stop. Get help.
3 Not only can blisters be painful, but infections can result and be literally life-threatening. Have them treated at an aid station.
4 If stretching does not relieve cramps, stop at an aid station.
5 Abrasions (skin scrapes, 'strawberries') may become infected. Have them treated.
Report significant injuries or downed runners to medical personnel. A field hospital will be established at the finish line. Injured runners will be transported there.

Prevention of Physical Problems

1 Runners attempting to participate in a race of this distance should have trained adequately. This should include at least two long-distance runs within the previous month that are at least two-thirds the length of this race.

2 Avoid running to exhaustion within the week preceding the race.

3 Remember, you will be running on yesterday's meals. We suggest a light meal no less than two hours before the race. Avoid fatty foods on race day. Emphasize carbohydrate intake the day before the race.

4 Maintenance of adequate hydration is the most important preventive measure. If you become thirsty, you are behind in fluids. Drink two 8-oz glasses of fluid (preferably water) within 10 to 15 minutes of race time. Drink continuously throughout the run. Unless you are totally committed to time, stop to drink; finishing is the goal. There will be water stations at the start as well as along the course.

5 Pre-run warm-up must include stretching exercises of the calf, hamstring, quadriceps, groin, and trunk muscles. If you begin to feel muscle tightness or cramps, stop and stretch.

6 Blisters can be prevented by wearing well-fitted, broken-in shoes and soft lightweight socks. Powder in shoes and socks will reduce friction. Remove pebbles immediately. Nails should be trimmed. If you feel a hot spot developing, stop at an aid station for care. They will be positioned every three miles.

7 Chafing occurs where clothing rubs against the skin. It can be prevented by wearing loose fitting clothing and applying petroleum jelly or protective bandaging in susceptible areas such as nipples, armpits, neckline, and groin.

8 You will be one of many runners, so run defensively. Stay to the left. Watch out for other runners and yield if necessary.

9 Pace yourself. Don't burn yourself out by starting too quickly. Common sense is the key.

The starting line is something I seldom notice. I go well back in the crowd, then we all start to move, slowly because there are so many out in front. There's a lot of nervously happy banter; we're nervous because deep down we're asking ourselves, "Are we going to stand up to all that pain ahead of us?" Once the crowd thins out, we begin to run faster, and introspection stops, for there are always cheering, supporting crowds. Marathon routes fascinate me, for there's so much to see, shop window styles, architecture, and later on when crowds have thinned, gardens and countryside. The Sunday morning crowds in Bermuda were definitely of the church-going fraternity, kind and warm-hearted. Running downhill to meet them was lovely. Running uphill, away, wasn't. But there was a welcome drinks stop just as we left downtown Hamilton and set out for the shore run. Roads on small islands are, of necessity, narrow, as there's no land to spare. When the roads were made, and land on either side sold, and stone walls built, the means of transport was by horse and carriage, with road width to suit.

Today's fast cars make running on the narrow roads a matter for caution and care, on both sides. There are strict regulations about who is allowed to have a car, and they don't apply to visitors, so taxis abound. I often had the feeling that they were family cars, which, when opportunity offered, were taxis. But they were always opulently comfortable.

In the early part of the marathon, there were no cars on the roads and we could run along, chatting. "I feel so safe running with you", I told my companion, a New York cop. "I feel safe with you because you're one of the six celebrities in the race." he answered. "You'll come to no harm, you'll be looked after." Just then, I began to feel discomfort in my left foot, and stopped to investigate, and he ran on. After that I was on my own. Unnoticed by me, two holes had appeared in the inner sole of my running shoe, something that could so easily have been put right by inserting another sole. But my fingers didn't feel the sole, and concentrated on smoothing out sock and shoe wall. I was baffled as to why there should be so much discomfort and pain after eight miles; so I kept on going and tried not to think about it. And foolishly didn't ask for help at an aid station.

We ran past Flatts township and made our way round Haringay Sound. As I passed a Baptist Church, some young girls came out and ran with me for a couple of miles. That was a real refreshment. On the far side of the Sound, was the half-way mark, and I looked around without joy. I was tired at every step. A man ran up to me, "Would you like orange juice?" and he ran down the long drive of his house, catching up with me in his car, a brimming glass of iced orange in his hand. The water tank lorry had been replenishing supplies at the drink stops was on its clearing up round. "Like a drink?" called the driver, and he made sure I was never short of water for the rest of the route.

My diary tells:

> They call it Bermuda. I call it Paradise. Tree-clad islands of volcanic origin, popping out of the crystal clear sea, palm trees fringing coves of pink sand, and hard, hard roads. Bermuda's must be the beautiful marathon.
>
> Perhaps I was too exhausted to continue with the diary, but continue with the marathon I did.

Coming along the South Shore (very close to the open Atlantic) had a tonic effect. By this time, I was a long way behind anyone else, but a young girl on a bicycle rode behind me, and told me which turnings to take. She was good company, and I wasn't carrying a map so I might easily have gone on running in the wrong direction. About 18 miles, a group of guests from my Bermudiana Hotel, brought me a bottle of Guinness and took photographs of me happily drinking it. On the route went, tantalisingly past the gorgeous looking pink Bermudiana, and up the hill beyond it. I had the impression that we only had a couple of miles to go to the stadium, and when directed to keep going straight ahead, I was sure my informant was wrong. My kind cyclist had gone by this time, so I stopped a couple of cars, but they had no idea of the route. I realised that to carry the map would have been sensible even if I couldn't read it. The motorists could have. New York has a blue painted line all along the route, Bermuda has the mileage total painted in yellow, on the road middle. (Why did they get so far apart after mile 18?) Then a lady motor cyclist came along as if on cue. She knew the route, and I followed her into the stadium. A little crowd had gathered to welcome me, and had even put up a finishing tape. I breasted that in style for the TV cameras, and sank into a car for the drive back to my hotel.

The hot bath in my beautiful Bermudiana bathroom after the race was bliss. However, hot water on an exposed blister was sharp agony.

Oh, the delight of lying back and being still. But coming in last meant there wasn't all that much time for getting into my gold sequin and white silk harem trousers evening dress and off by taxi to the Elbow Beach Hotel for the prizegiving. But it was worth hurrying for.

There was a dazzling array of prizes, and, as with everything in Bermuda, the presentations were done with style. TV cameras, dazzling lights, the media in full force. The Governor of the island presented the prizes with charm and the dignity of his office. The race sponsors, Adidas and Eastern Airlines were joined in generosity by *Athlete's World* in providing gifts of clothes, cups and trophies.

The Bermuda Track & Field Association together with Eastern Airlines provided a handsome Bermudian cedarwood goblet, which I won, as second Female Senior Master, the tactful American way of saying 'veteran'. Evelyn Havers who had beaten me by six minutes in New York, had done it again, by an hour and ten minutes this time.

The Bermuda Marathon

She wasn't there to receive her prizes, but I was given a handsome silver cup from *Athlete's World*, presented by Mrs. Bruce Ayling, the editor's pretty wife, as well as a smart Adidas shower jacket, so Eve's must have been even better.

The only prizes I'd ever won for sport, gave me a real thrill. And the cedarwood cup had a special interest. In 1944, a juniper bush was brought to the island, as an added interest item in a garden. Unknown and unseen, it harboured a tiny insect, which settled on the cedarwood trees and proliferated. So much so, that the cedars began to die out. The island had been plentifully supplied with these handsome trees. At one time in its history, it was the home of successful sea-raiders (or pirates) and it was said that the cedarwood constructed ships that slid so easily through the water, helped them to win their spoils of victory. Since those days, cedarwood was used in housebuilding and furniture, and the loss of the trees was a serious matter for a national industry.

The Department of Agriculture and Fisheries have been studying the problem and taking counter measures such as growing cedars immune to the ravages of the pest. So far, they have not had much success.

Back to the excitements of *aprés* marathon at Elbow Beach. Grete Waitz was there at the prizegiving, elegant in beige and brown, but as I made my way to meet her, people kept coming to congratulate me. "Hold one of my cups and we'll have a photo", said Ray Swan, always cool, the top Bermudian runner, fifteenth overall and winner of the Masters Division. He handed me a cup, almost big enough to bath a baby in; my own cup was just the right size for a flower arrangement.

I had given the man who came in second last (and an hour before me) a big disappointment. There's a cult of 'coming in last' in America. He'd thought I was sure to be one of the 68 people who gave up out of the 300 starters. "Madge, I'm proud of you", and a distinguished looking Fred Lebow (organiser of the New York Marathon) kissed me on the lips. That he should recognise me, let alone praise me was a great thrill. A voice came from the crowd, "Well done." "But I was last", I wailed. "And stole the show."

The blister on my foot was worrying me now, and hurting. I still don't know why I didn't avail myself of the help offered me by first aid workers at the end of the marathon. I suppose I just didn't want to bother anyone with anything as small and unimportant as a blister. How wrong that thinking was came home to me pretty soon, when it became swollen and inflamed. I went to the local hospital next morning, and had it dressed. "Salt water will be good for it", the doctor told me, "of course you can swim."

So I went on by bus to Horseshoe Bay, a lovely curve of sand on the South Shore, where I swam , and had a little sleep in the warm sunshine. Two young men who had run in the marathon, recognised me from my articles in *Running* and joined me. They were very sensibly staying on with friends working on the islands, to make a proper holiday of the trip. We went by bus to the westward end of the islands, Somerset, where they stayed, and had a welcome tea.

I brought out my autograph book, a present from Ewen M. Stewart of Prince Edward Island, whom I'd met while watching the 10km. race. "Great to meet you in Bermuda, keep on getting the miles in. Kind regards" wrote Dave Mellor from Derby. Dave had ridden the Land's End to John o' Groats cycle run in 1978. His friend, Stuart Walker, also of Charnwood A.C. wrote, "Best Wishes to the Best Runner in the UK. May you compete in many more marathons. It's great to run in the same race as you. Hope to see you at Peking Marathon." Well, perhaps one day.

Ewen had shown me his own autograph book, a mass of close signatures, and I thought it such a good idea to turn an A4 size book (just a small piece of printing and a drawing of runners on each of the pages, printed on one side only) into something very personal, and yet a memory of each marathon I run. I take it to special events, broadcasting and TV as well as marathons and sporting events, and now it's one of my most precious possessions.

After the marathon, the Bermudiana gave a swizzle stick party before dinner (such a delightful way for guests to be introduced to each other) and we consumed quantities of a delicious rum based drink. Bill McBay of Wakefield, Ma. had come to Bermuda for a break, to ease the pain of the first anniversary of his wife's death. He had been an American Air Force pilot in the Second World War, and knew Britain fairly well. We had a lot in common, and dined together after that evening. Life in Hamilton after dinner seemed extremely quiet, unless you were of a mind to go to late late nightclubs. Walking along Front Street, looking at the beautiful displays of jewellery, furniture, cashmeres and porcelain was pleasure enough. Bermuda is a showcase for the best merchandise in the world, since cruise liners dock on one side of the street, right opposite the shops. It must be the most attractive dockland there is, with a line of gardens to conceal the security fencing.

We boarded a ferryboat, that went off across the bay, touching in at islands in the same way as it must have done since the islands became inhabited. In the darkness, lights flashing over the rippling water it all looked incredibly romantic. By next morning, I was off at first light to appear on 'Good Morning Bermuda', a friendly chat show.

The inflammation on my foot was anything but romantic and I returned to the hospital. "You've got sand underneath the skin", said a doctor, "and I'm going to cut it off." He did, and it not only hurt then, but every time I put my foot on the ground. "Yes", he said, "salt water and exposure to the sun will do it good." So I made my way back to Horseshoe Bay and swam. As I made my painful way up the hill from the beach to the main road, a man on a moped drew up beside me. "Hop on the pillion", he said, "I've left my wife at the top. We couldn't let you walk up this hill, and you can get a bus at the top back to Hamilton and your hotel." As I waited for the bus, the pain was so acute that I thumbed a lift and asked to be dropped near the hospital. Of course they took me right there, and a doctor cut off more skin, and I was given a stout walking stick with a rubber end. I find it most useful now, for swishing back my lounge curtains.

Swimming was out, and walking was out too. I phoned room service in the hotel, "May I have a wheelchair?" That was better. Bill wheeled me down for dinner and a moonlit walk around the grounds. We were going home next day so I didn't miss much in the way of swimming. After he'd gone, I decided I'd go out on my own and buy some black rum in a nearby supermarket. Wheelchairs need a little getting used to, and I faced a downhill slope with some trepidation. But I needn't have worried. A lady crossed over to me, "Let me help you". How kind she was, wheeling me back up that steepish hill, both of us weighted with bottles of black (the strongest) rum. Yes, it tasted good with ginger as a 'dark and stormy' drink. Of course, the ginger ale is the best in the world, grown on Barbados and freshly made. The two make a really good combination.

After dinner, I drank my last sundowner on my balcony and said goodbye to those beautiful islands. They looked so serene and comfortable, all the people I saw, so very well dressed. At that time, in '82, the average annual income per person with family was £6,000. But there were rumblings of troubles underneath. Sir Richard Sharples had been murdered back in 1971 and that had never been explained.

I sat in the hotel waiting for Clive Longhe (the administrator of the marathon) who was very kindly sending a taxi to drive me to the airport. "It's been lovely", I said to Billy, the hotel's security officer, "I think I like Horseshoe Bay best of all." "We've lost one or two tourists there", he informed me. I was glad I hadn't known. "Youse the best known person on the island", said my waiter, "everywheres ah go, theyse talkin' 'bout you." And I think I've been talking about them ever since.

17 Winchester marathon and 'The Place', Hanley

My arrival home was dramatic. Our plane was late and I arrived at Adam's wedding lunch, with my injured foot in a sock and two plastic bags to keep out the cold. The family rushed outside. As I rather slowly got out of the taxi, half the guests were observing my arrival. Preparations for the next marathon would need to be delayed. My daughter-in-law, Barbara, looked lovely.

The hospital doctor in Bermuda had cut away the skin from the sole of my foot, so that every time I put my weight on it, recovery was hindered. At least, so I reasoned. But it did heal, cleanly, and I started running again, for we had Winchester's marathon and half marathon on 14 March.

That was a snowy winter, 1982. Before Bermuda, I'd been out running on roads narrowed by snow thrown up at the sides by the snowplough. As more snow fell, the roads narrowed further, until I felt it was dangerous to run, with traffic passing and spraying up slush. Very early on Sunday mornings was a good time to get out, and I liked my Pony shoes, with a very good tread, to keep me from skidding.

As the snow disappeared in town, it was still lying high by the roadsides out in the country. Mornings were sparklingly clear and sunny. Running in the crisply cold air made you feel glad to be alive and able to get out to enjoy it.

I decided that to train enough to run the full Winchester marathon, might put the London at risk on 13 May, so I only ran a half. But that was a big surprise. Winchester people came out in their hundreds and cheered with as much enthusiasm as anywhere else. Perhaps even more, since there was a 'hometown intimacy'. It was a beautiful route. Every King and Queen of England and Britain has walked Winchester's streets. The following two articles appeared in the *Hampshire Chronicle*:

A Message from Madge

Winchester's best-known veteran long-distance runner, Madge Sharples, writes: "We're keyed up now, ready for the fray on Sunday. If it's any consolation, thousands of Chinese are in the same position – the Shanghai Marathon is run on March 14th! Carbo-loading on a Chinese diet may have presented a few problems. I hope you're well rested, not too lightly clad, for March winds can be unkind and make you thirsty.

"It's such a beautiful route. Think, as you run up Three Maids Hill, of the story of the three maidens, who helped an escaping highwayman by feeding him, and for their punishment, were buried up to their necks, and left to starve to death. You've a drinks station coming soon after. On to Crawley, the old Crawanlea (Glade of the Crows) past its charming pond with teal and merganser. You'll be heading back towards Winchester, having passed the highest part of the route just before Crawley; a quick mile and a half to the right turn on to the old Andover-road, wooded on either side, where our Forces were drawn up, waiting, ready for D-Day.

"Past the roundabout, and on to Down Farm-lane, yes, it's almost all down from here, down to the watercress beds and interesting waterfowl. (An acre of watercress needs one million gallons of water every two-and-a-half hours, at a constant temperature of 50–51°, from springs that run all the year round, over stones, to which the roots cling.)

"Now there's only the Worthy-road between you and the finish. You may be running too fast to take in the details of the little gem of a Saxon Church, St. Swithun's. But you will appreciate the comforts of Winchester Recreation Centre, the plaudits of the crowd and the fun of being one of a throng of like-minded, single-minded people.

Togetherness

That sums up the Winchester Mayor's Marathon. (And didn't he do well?) It was a perfect day for the slower runners, with some strong wind, but the fast élite coped. Barry Watson's 2.22.33 full marathon win was a triumph for that hilly course, and Ian Ray's 1.1.05 was a spectacular half marathon win. Nothing spectacular about my 2.28.14, 615th out of the field of 905 finishers for the half marathon, but what I'll remember to my dying day, is the warmth and friendliness of the runners, and the cheers of the onlookers, friends all.

To think that as we half marathoners plodded up the Littleton–Crawley road, one of the two leaders of the full marathon took time to give me a wee hug, turn around and greet me. From then on, as the 781 who completed the full course, ran past me, it was hand clappings and greetings all the way: "Darling Madgie, keep going love, like your top, you're doing fine, Pet, read your column." I hadn't breath to answer them all, but I'll never forget them. We were all there, striving, together.

And the finish, that madly abandoned sprint down the last 50 metres, the happiness of meeting so many smiling faces, being interviewed by John Kane and gazing bemusedly into a TV camera lens as if it had nothing to do with me; being presented with an exquisite bouquet of flowers by Mrs. Grace Oram's little daughter, on behalf of Highcliffe Community Association (for whose Building Fund I was running) celebrating the day with wine in Nun's Road with Peter and fellow Wessex joggers, as we cheered on the four hours plus finishers. Happiness isn't perfect until it's shared.

Winchester, we didn't set you on fire; it was your warm glow that fuelled us on to the finish. And we want to thank you, officials all and the host of unnamed helpers: police, wardens, timekeepers, first aiders, drinks and sponge station servers, messengers, CB radio and John Kane and Bob Iles who kept us so well informed. All your efforts knitted us into a community of TOGETHERNESS.

Hampshire Chronicle, May, 1981.

April 7 – A note from my diary:

Off to Stoke-on-Trent to speak at the marathon club, the gem of a bright idea, run by Kevin Donovan and Don Shelley. Trains busy, people standing, and bulging suitcases everywhere. If Jimmy Savile can do training runs on trains, he must travel very early or late. People were bulging like their suitcases, munching contentedly. My compartment neighbour was reading 'The magic of thinking BIG'. When he stopped to eat his lunch, I asked could I have a peep at it. "No, I'm reading it", he very properly replied, with all the defiant truculence of a small boy.

Pretty country all the way; after Oxford, mellow stone houses with stone slates – 'presents' I believe they're called. Approaching the Potteries, the 'Black' country, I looked for smoke stacks, kilns, soot blackened buildings. Arnold Bennett's novel *Five Towns*, which I won as a prize at school, is still fresh in my mind. I'm almost expecting to meet a 1980s version of 'The Card'. But here are cows browsing, green arable country. Stone and Wedgwood lie in country as rural as you could wish, blossom bedecked hedges, rich pasture lands. Handsome is the word for the Palladian-style Stoke station with stone half-pillars. A man was sweeping up with the broadest brush I've ever seen, but very little to sweep up. To be met at the station by Don Shelley and escorted to my hotel (the Stafford County, THF) right across the road from the station, was kindness indeed. I could simply have been given the address. Real North Country hospitality.

Out to get the flavour of Stoke – Technical College Library open to the public – that's good. Nail varnish bought from a chemist at half the price in Winchester. Good too. Back for a sizzling hot bubble bath in my private bathroom, bigger than many a bedroom, made even more delightful by having a pot of tea, which I didn't need at all, alongside. Dressed for dinner in my sportiest outfit.

Don drove me to Kevin Donovan's leisure centre in Hanley, 'The Place'. Frilly shirted young men in evening dress, who reminded me of Steve Davis, greeted us at the entrance. It certainly added tone, as did the opulently carpeted and furnished wide open arena where the marathon club was to meet. Drinks at a bar, shaded lights, varied seating, a sports shop in the background, soft music, video screen at the ready. Everything laid on in a most tasteful, discreet way. The video of Desmond Lynam interviewing me before the New York marathon (Oct. '81) was put on as an introduction, and I found myself on stage, in a brilliant light, mike on stand before me. But where was the audience? The front row melted into an area of darkness. It was an odd feeling. Was I talking to Dinosaurs or what?

But I got on with my talk. Memorising headings is a good way to avoid that 'sudden cliff fall into blankness' that a mike on an empty floodlit stage could bring. I worked my way through my intro – the 'two-F's': Flexibility and Fresh Air – going on to demonstrate some stretching exercises and Belly Breathing, with a few anecdotes tossed in. Odd how, when I expect good laughter, there's a polite murmur, and when I'm not expecting it at all, there's a roar. Such as my acting the part of the widow in Terence Rattigan's 'Separate Tables'. "You brought the house down," I was told. But it wasn't a funny part at all.

I had no idea of the time I'd been speaking, but sensed I ought to stop, and asked for questions. None came, so I continued speaking, as if answering some. At last there were some words of thanks, and loud applause that went on and on. "That's the most applause we've had for any speaker", said Don. "They must have liked what you said." It was quite embarrassing standing there on the stage in the lights, without seeing the audience. What on earth do other people do? I smiled, looked bashful and left the stage. A queue of men had formed. "Madge, will you sign your article in *Running* Magazine?" Several had brought a copy of 'The Marathon Guide' (written and published by Don Shelley and Kevin Donovan) and I signed that, wondering if there was going to be room for the more important authors' signatures as well on the flyleaf.

In to the Marathon Office, specially built, to see the card index of information for next year's Marathon Guide, and back to the hotel. A really good evening. Somehow, it had gone so smoothly, I felt I hadn't done enough work to earn all this friendly adulation, if that's not too strong a word.

A good morning phone call, a foamy bath and an excellent breakfast. Then Don took me past the very fine Palladian Town Hall, an architectural gem, to John Bourne's sports shop nearby. An alchemist's cave of brightly coloured treasures of sports wear. What a comprehensive stock. All framed by blue and green carpeting and blue upholstered benches. Smart.

John had just run seven miles, and was showering, his brother told us. But he came along and presented me with a copy of Kelvin Bowers' *Closing the Distance* (about travelling to Australia by land) an enthralling tale of effort surmounting obstacles. A universal story with an example that could be applied to any kind of life, and a thoughtful and kind gift from John Bourne.

Don dropped me off at Stoke Museum. That name is too prosaic, it's a treasure house – slides of wild flowers, trees, Roman and Elizabethan coins, stuffed animals, ladies in 17th-century costume. I hastened past the 20th-century display when I saw a model wearing a dress, the neighbour of which I wore happily for years; then, upstairs to see what I'd come specially to see – the ironstone, pottery, porcelain and bone china exhibits. I noted how they were made, then moved on to ornamental ceramics.

A Victorian credo was, to make useful things beautiful. Today, they are simply quaint objects. Those in Japanese-style were both elegant and simple, in soft colours. Perhaps the object that appealed to me most, was a glass bowl, treated to look like ivory, with Japanese-style tracery in gold. Warm, delicate, useful, perhaps, but beautiful.

Left Stoke by train for Birmingham, with young people in the compartment, who recognised me. One had a radio cassette so I let him play my tape of the NY marathon. Called on sports shops in Birmingham and got two possible orders for Valerie Tehel of Poole for her knitted woolly hats.

On to Leamington Spa, where the widow of grandmother's cousin, Sir James Weir was killed as she got out of her car on the wrong side. Her chauffeur was opening the door on the other side, but Lady Noble (she had re-married by this time) was knocked down and killed. I walked down the Parade, past the colonnaded pump room by the river, fountains playing on a lake well populated by ducks and swans who ignored the whistle-blowing custodian. On to the train again to Reading and Winchester. Evening sunlight on pollarded willows is lovely. *Closing the Distance* is a marvellous book. An inspiration. Perhaps mine could be too?

18 The Second London Marathon

People were coming up to me as I made my way to the station, "Good luck Madge." "I'm thrilled", I answered, "I'm going to meet Salazar." Blank faces. They didn't know Alberto Salazar, the fastest marathon runner in the world. Chris Gates of Guinness met me at Waterloo, and we drove to the Cobra Sports shop near the old Covent Garden.

Photographers and reporters were crammed in a downstairs room. On a chair in the centre, rather like 'Mastermind', was a young, fresh-faced Salazar, fawn showerproof jacket, dark trousers and new Nike shoes. He sat, answering a stream of non-stop questions. Andy Etchells was there firing his from the iron spiral staircase leading down to the interview room. "Why aren't you running in the London?" Alberto had an air of straightforward innocence. "Well, the London's pretty near the track season. I like to limit my roadracing to two or three races a year. I prefer to be ready for track and cross country." A photographer approached me, "We want you and Alberto together after the questions".

So there we were, sitting on a velvet chair chatting. It seemed incredible, that one year ago, I was the most frightened, hesitant runner who ever faced up to a marathon. And yet here I was happily chatting with the world's best, before the press. Life can do some pretty marvellous turn-ups.

"Will you kiss him?" asked the photographers. "And again, and again." "Now", they continued to Alberto this time, "will you kneel in front of Madge and tie her shoe lace." And he did this, with the best grace and sweetest smile in the world. A true champion. "Let Madge put her 'Marathon Madge' cap on you." And he did. Afterwards, he joined his pretty young wife who was waiting in a taxi and off they went.

Through the good offices of Anthony Smith (Manager of Winchester's Wessex Hotel) Harold Krushandl, of the Cavendish

Hotel, London, had invited me to be a guest of the Trust House Forte management for the marathon. The invitation had taken the form of an offer of accommodation at the hotel. So, just to be prepared for picnic lunches in my bedroom for economy's sake, I'd taken a lump of cheese and some butter with me. When I went to the hotel desk to register, after Chris had driven me from the Cobra shop, I was asked to wait for a moment. Harold welcomed me with Austrian kisses and Sue Kershaw, trainee manager, took me up to see my room where roses and carnations and a bowl of the most luscious fruit, big bottle of Moet & Chandon, Première Cuvée were awaiting me. I suggested opening the champagne there and then, but that was waved away. We went down to a lounge bar and had two rounds of champagne there, chatting with other guests, then off into the beautiful dining room for a wonderful lunch.

The Cavendish Hotel was actually the home of the 'Duchess of Duke Street' of TV series fame. She was a real favourite of Edward the Seventh and an oil painting of her, tall, statuesque and beautiful, hangs in the hall of the Cavendish. It's not an ordinary hotel, so beautifully furnished and with such discreet, attentive service, staying there gives you the feeling that you are a guest in a mansion. I was a guest, with a perfect host.

After lunch, I had to go to Lilleywhites, where a beautiful Schiaparelli (shocking) pink Atlas Leisuresuit was ready for me, with 'Lilleywhites' in large letters across the back. There was a matching pink silk running outfit, vest and shorts as well, but I'd agreed to run wearing 'Madge Loves Cavendish Hotel', printed on a white cotton T-shirt. The delightful pink silk outfit came in useful later on. I don't think people quite cottoned on to the drawing of the heart meaning 'love'. They were shouting, "Come on Madge Cavendish," at the marathon. Back to the Hotel with my lovely packages, and after some tea, dressed in the Atlas pink leisure suit.

I taxied across to the London Weekend TV studios to take part in the 6 o'clock show, and was shown into a enormous hall, like a circus ring, with steeply banked rows of seats for the studio audience. There was a bigger surprise than ever for me, for I was led to the front row of seats and placed beside Jimmy Savile, resplendent in his gold lamé running outfit. "How happy I am to meet you", I gasped and he responded with a big kiss on the lips. Leslie Watson looking lovelier than ever was in the row behind, and in came Chris Brasher. Another big kiss. I was feeling quite at home, and set about getting some autographs.

Alberto Salazar had written that morning, "Good luck in your running," and Chris Brasher added, "To Madge whose smile started millions of people running, with love Chris Brasher".

"Keep on doing those P.B's. Love, Leslie Watson".

"Love 2 Marvellous Madge, from Jimmy Savile xxx."

"Best Wishes, Alan Minter."

"Good times always, Roddy McDonald."

"With Love for your love of running, Harry, Tony and all at the Cavendish."

"Please God let me be in front of Madge, John Robinson, Blackheath Harriers."

As the cameras began to roll, Michael Aspel ran in breathless to introduce the programme. There was to be a Marathon Phone-in, with well known actors and actresses answering the telephones ranged round the floor of the hall. The studio audience consisted of specially invited marathon runners and in lulls between phone calls, celebrity runners were to be interviewed. And the cause of all this, was an appeal to raise money for Leukaemia Research.

Sometimes, the generous people phoning in couldn't believe that they were really talking to the Stars. "It's me, Lulu", a radiant Lulu was shouting, "Yes, really". Michael kept tabs on the amounts of money being promised and excitement rose as the thousands rolled in. Fred Housego ex-taxidriver 'Mastermind' was shown on a TV screen, describing the marathon route from a helicopter. Appetites were whetted for Race Day. In all, £80,000 was promised for a very worthy cause.

Leaving the studio – on my way to meet Adam and Barbara at an upstairs reception – I was delighted to meet Bob Wiseman's wife.

He was going to run in the marathon, but couldn't make it to the charity event. We enjoyed the drinks and chatter at the reception, all runners and TV people. If I didn't know many, quite a number seemed to know me. "When are you coming to run in Jersey?" I haven't forgotten, and would like to come one year, when the date doesn't clash with other events that I've promised to take part in.

Then, back to the Cavendish for dinner. Adam couldn't believe that we were actually guests of the management, and was nervously choosing the least expensive wine. He felt sure he'd end up paying for our evening. But though the bill came to £82 for the dinner, it was on the house, and we had a lovely evening.

Next morning, 100 per cent thrilled with everything, but still finding about 50 per cent fright deep down at the thought of the sheer pain that the 26 miles inflict, I strolled along to the Piccadilly Hotel. The Cavendish, on the corner of Duke Street and Jermyn Street, is in the most perfect position in London. It's so quiet, yet so near Piccadilly and Trafalgar Square. Registration for the London marathon was taking place in the Piccadilly Hotel, so I joined the crowds. In the bright sunshine, everyone seemed to be on top of the world. Fred Lebow was there, and kissed me – instant recognition, unless he kisses every girl he meets and I don't think he does. What am I saying "girl!"

The Greater London Council
present
The 1982 Gillette London Marathon

Dear Marathon Aspirant,

Many of you will have been part of the 1981 Marathon – either as a runner or spectator or helper or even as a tele-watcher. So first, a profound thank you, to all of you who entered into the spirit of the event: it was a great adventure, a day which proved that the human spirit is indomitable. Last year we said that the future of the event depended on every single competitor being a considerate competitor, prudent pedestrian and cheerful colleague. And you were – so now we have permission to stage another great festival on Sunday May 9th, 1982. Details of how to enter are on the reverse side of this letter. They may sound rigid and pedantic but we only have a very small part-time staff to handle thousands of applications and we want to keep it that way because we now have charitable status and we want to keep our costs to a bare minimum so that we can hand over as much money as possible for the improvement of recreation facilities in inner-city areas – something that is much needed these days.

So we try to automate our entry handling system with the aid of British Olivetti computers and envelope stuffing machines. Hence the insistence on standard size envelopes (9" by 4") and only one entry per envelope.

We have tried to make the entry system as fair as possible and the Post Office will help by sorting the envelopes according to time and date of posting – not time of delivery.

So you will help us greatly by entering exactly as instructed and by refraining from writing or telephoning us. And please, no stories about the baby/dog/cat eating your entry form. This year we came to the conclusion that Britain's babies had forsaken their normal diet and taken, exclusively, to a liking for Marathon entry forms.

The route for 1982 will be substantially the same as 1981 which produced the fastest ever times – for both men and women – of any marathon ever held in England. We shall iron out some kinks and bottlenecks and greatly improve the finish.

We shall also try to make the whole weekend into a festival: there will be a pasta party on Saturday May 8th, and Sunday night the prizegiving will be followed by dancing and jollification. Registration next year will be at the Piccadilly Hotel (about 100 yards from Eros) and will open on Thursday May 6th. We shall have much more room and there will be meeting places, seminars on many aspects of marathon running, a trade show and you will even be able to have your feet attended to by trained chiropodists!

May your training go well and good luck to you all.

Chris Brasher	*John Disley*	*Derrick Pollard*
Race Director	Course Director	Administration Director

Registration for any marathon is always exciting. A time to meet old friends and make new, see sportswear displays, sample electrolyte drinks and discuss the route. At the London, runners have come from every corner of Britain, and some from distant parts of the world, so I was kept busy, signing programmes and standing in family groups for photographs. The Trouble Desk can't have been busy; at least, Derrick Pollard, Alan Sawyer and Eric James found time to sign my autograph book.

Back to the Cavendish for lunch, and then off by taxi to take part in BBC's 'Sport on 2'. As we passed the Piccadilly Hotel, the queue which began in the downstairs registration hall, had spread out into the street, and went all round the block. Some people stood for two-and-a-half hours. But at least it was sunny and warm, and everyone seemed very good humoured. The studio I was taken to was below ground and pretty warm, but a fascinating hive of industry. Wearing earphones, amply supplied with coffee and sandwiches, I was able to watch both BBC 2 and ITV. People were dashing in with messages to be relayed.

I sat, stretching my legs under a table that held my microphone, and worked at the quadriceps strengthening exercises – straighten out the legs, on a level with your chair, push extra hard to extend the heels as much as possible, and feel the tension go right up the backs of your legs to your buttocks. Hold for five seconds, release for three and repeat again and again.

At intervals, I spoke a little about running generally and this London marathon in particular. I had imagined I would be on the air for a few minutes and then say, "Goodbye," but no, 'Sport on 2' is an afternoon-long occasion. "When you think of the famous people who've been on this programme, it's something to be on it." said Mike Ingham, the announcer. "I'll give you a list of their names."

When relaxation was the order of the day, at the end, Mike signed my autograph book, "Thank you for being such a 'Sport on 2'" and Bryan Tremble wrote "Thanks for being such a lovely guest on 'Sport on 2', lovely to meet you." Yes, it was a great way to spend a pre-marathon afternoon, nerves completely driven away by seeing footballers buzzing about like flies, cyclists panting, swimmers and more footballers, rugby, and peaceful looking snooker. I came away with a heightened admiration for the truly able radio commentators. And on the way back to the Cavendish, there was still a queue outside the Piccadilly Hotel waiting to register.

Off to the pasta party at the Royal Lancaster Hotel; up Park Lane, past Marble Arch and along Bayswàter Road. London looking so fresh and clean; streets romantically different in the soft evening light. Budding trees were like drifts of green lace. The very street names are magic, Duke St., St James's, Arlington St., Burlington Gardens, Bruton St., Savile Row.

The Royal Lancaster Hotel was a seething mass of runners and their families. I was taken at once to Ron Pickering, who was on a central platform, and introduced as "The nation's sweetheart who has firmly established herself as the No. 1 lady of the marathon". There was tremendous clapping and grasping a mike, I turned round to say a few words, "It's thanks to you that I've gone on running. It's the feedback from your encouragement that has enabled me to run at the Peoples, Chelmsley Wood, North Tyneside at Whitley Bay, New York, Bermuda and Winchester."

Ron Pickering spoke of his pal Clive Longhe in Bermuda. Had he treated me well? Of course. Tall, and handsome as a film star, athletic Clive, with his charming ways and perfect manners made me feel like a queen. Yes, Yes, of course. I enlarged on the delights of the islands, running round the bays of pink sands watching shoals of fish swimming in clearest water, waves breaking invigoratingly on the South Shore. The audience was quiet. I climbed down to roars of applause and started signing autographs. "Madge will be signing autographs for the next two hours", said Ron I was, almost.

"You can always break records on Record Pasta", wrote Paul Sugdon (MD of Record Pasta). I was taken off to take part in the video being made of the pasta party in general and some guests in particular. And more autographs, photos, kisses.

Leslie Watson came then, and went through the Ron Pickering podium treatment. We all loved to hear her speak about running. Just as well she wasn't there to hear me being called No. 1 lady of the marathon. At last there was a pause on the rostrum, "Are there any fellow geriatrics here?" I asked Ron. One hand shot up – a man of 66 running in the marathon with his daughter. "It's so relaxing", he told me. Well, up to a certain stage, yes.

As I stood by the podium, they were running the video of the first London Marathon. I could see myself being interviewed at the end by Tony Gubba. How rapturously happy I looked. "Must get a copy of that", I thought.

My shocking pink Atlas track suit, 'Lilleywhites' printed across the back, couldn't have been bettered for jumping on a podium with an audience of thousands. What an experience; what a weekend. So much good fellowship, so few women, so few grey hairs; so much smiling banter, "Wait for me, Madge".

Came out to crowds of well-wishers saying, "Good luck," and came back to the quiet Cavendish. I can see why New Yorkers love to come to London. It's such a compact gathering of all they want to see, theatres, shops, fine and ancient buildings, art galleries, museums and royalty. It's a liqueur of a city.

I came down to the dining room to do a little more carbo-loading. Chose rice and scampi. A morsel of sole was cooked specially for me. The chef sent in a photograph of the staff team from Trust House Forte (who ran in the London–Brighton race) for my autograph. More like me getting his. Food in the Cavendish is superb, to the last detail, and those creamy gateaux. But before the marathon, I stuck to fresh fruit and melon, though I was really too excited to eat. I admired the long-stemmed red roses and a candle, on each table, lovely red azaleas in full flower in copper tubs on mantelpieces, some hanging plants, modern paintings, soft piano music live, and a happy hum of chinking cutlery and china, laughter and voices.

"Music when soft voices die, vibrates in the memory," wrote Shelley.

My diary records:

Why does it take so long to get ready, the night before a marathon? The pins for the running number, pound note folded into a sock leg, tissues folded ready, though these aren't much worth if it rains, plasters ready cut; are my socks OK, shoes free of creases at the toe joint (that blister-vulnerable spot) what weight and warmth of running shorts will tomorrow's temperature require? But it was May 9th, and we could expect pleasant warmth. By 11 p.m. I could relax, or try to. I know the experts say: "Get extra sleep before a marathon!", but how can you, tossing and turning and on a warm night too.

The latest advice is to 'do' something the night before, go to the cinema or have a drink with friends at a pub. Then, diverted and relaxed by having your mind taken off the race, you'll sleep. But I still think that being stretched out in bed, whether awake or asleep, from an early hour, is best. But I'll have a good book with me next time.

Up at 1 a.m.; up at 3 a.m. At least I didn't wash my hair at 3 a.m. as I did in my Milford Plaza Hotel bedroom, before the New York marathon. 6 a.m. call and breakfast in bed. Prunes, All Bran, boiled egg, so soft it was almost liquid, just as I like it, brown toast, honey and tea. Ready for the off at 7 a.m.

Walking to Charing Cross station, down Pall Mall, swarms of empty taxis were rushing westwards, lemming-like. What could be happening beside the marathon at that early hour? Charing Cross was a moving mass of people. We all had rail tickets for specific trains. My 7.28 indicator said Dartford. "Will this stop at Greenwich?" I asked the ticket collector anxiously. "Are you sure?" Much laughter from round about. Marathon madness must be affecting me.

The train was packed, but near the front, there was an empty seat beside Bob from Wales. "I kept it for you", he said. Greenwich Station platform was jam-packed with people trying to get off, as we arrived, and some took 20 minutes. Our compartment was opposite the exit. "If we join in here, it's jumping the queue. Won't we sit still for a bit?" "And get carried on to Deptford?"

We were soon off and walking up to Greenwich Park. Autographs and photos. It was good to be so early and relaxed. 'Curios and Antiques' said a shop front. Gosh, don't rub it in. At the first London Marathon, the park just seemed an immense space of grass. But that was seen in March rain. It was a different place in May sunshine, everything so fresh and green.

I was delighted to meet Chris Brasher and John Disley in their smart plum and silver Goretex suits. The warmth of their welcome set the day for fair; sick apprehension diminished. The milling crowds were like a huge fairground. All we needed was hurdy gurdy music and a few chair-o-planes. But we were off on our personal planes pretty soon.

Registration particulars taken, Nescafé on offer, a visit to the portaloos and the belongings buses lined alphabetically in a long row, a positive fleet, and I lined up at the 4 hours 30 minutes billboard. If there were 8,000 runners in the Red Start, where I was, there were thousands of well wishers to see us off. It was a marvellous multi-coloured sight. Runners bobbing up and down, groin stretching, touching toes, hailing friends, laughing and talking. The very air seemed charged with energy, determination, will power, call it what you like. I wondered if sick people were brought there to see and share, might not some of the strength spread to them?

Could marathon starts become a new form of Lourdes? All our training is a testament of love and devotion to the Life Force, to God himself. Runners help each other in need; the organisers, police, traffic wardens, drinks servers, first aiders, physiotherapists, time-keepers, medal presenters – all help the runners. And the sum total is money – raised for charities. Marathons are a token expression of human goodness.

I was running in the Muscular Dystrophy Group of Great Britain Team captained by Harry Carpenter. Celebrity runners included:

Celebrities Running/Supporting the Muscular Dystrophy Group in the 1982 Gillette London Marathon

Alan Minter	Former World Middleweight Boxing Champion.
David Cropper	Olympic Athlete.
and his wife Pat	Olympic Gold Medallist.
David Lloyd	Davis Cup Tennis Player 1976/79
Ian McLauchlan	Former Scottish Rugby International.
Madge Sharples	Aged 65, oldest runner in this team.

Andy Follett	Youngest runner in the Marathon (18 years on May 8th)
Dr.J.P.R.Williams	Welsh and British Lion Rugby Player
Roger Uttley	Former Rugby International, Captain of England.
Gary Waller	Conservative MP, Brighouse and Spenborough.
Dick Douglas	Labour/Co-op. MP, Dunfermline.
Matthew Parris	Conservative MP, Derbyshire West.
Leslie Watson	World 50 mile record holder.

The gun for the start of the marathon went off with a soft boom, and we waited for instructions. When you're one of so many thousands lined up in the space of a park roadway, you have to go with the crowd. Then "Walk" boomed a voice from the loud speakers, "Jog" and "Stop". It was ten minutes before we reached the start, and turned at a right angle into the roadway proper. The crowds were still shouting and cheering us – good lung power there. The sheer mass of bodies kept everyone at a comfortably easy jog, with much chatter and laughter. Joe, from Wales, who'd run a marathon the week before, was a reassuring figure beside me. He wore cotton gloves that made him easily identifiable out of the corner of my eye. If he was still there, then I wasn't falling behind. Or so I thought. "I'll run with you to Tower Bridge", he said, "and then I'll race you to the finish." A born diplomat.

Running in the sunshine was a delight. Plenty of space now, with the comforting soft thud of runners behind, and the even more comforting cheers of the onlookers. "I deafened you as you passed the Cutty Sark" said a man at the Covent Garden Jamboree that night. It was wonderful "Madge, Madge", a tremendous roar, "There she is". "It's Madge", I only heard "There's that old woman from last year," once.

At the start of a marathon, I hear people shout, "There's the – ". As I slow down, at least I have the satisfaction of knowing what they're calling me. In Scotland, at the Edinburgh marathon, sometimes it was just a pitying "Aah . . ." I wanted to say, "Where's a mirror, do I really look as bad as that?"

As I ran towards Tower Bridge, a lady presented me with a beautiful white carnation, done up with maidenhair fern and silver foil, a lovely gesture. Where the crowds were gathered thickly at street corners, the deafening roar almost seemed to lift me off my feet, and I all but pirouetted along. At one point, a man leapt from the crowd, seized my arms and we danced a kind of polka to the music of cheers. Moments of purest magic. Perhaps this is a touch of what soldiers must feel, coming home from war.

Patches of the route were familiar. The long straight stretches, shining wet last year, didn't seem so long in the sunshine. Near the river, I sat down to investigate an unfunny feeling in my shoe – I was determined not to be so cussedly stupid as to bash on regardless, as I did in Bermuda, where a blood soaked shoe was my reward. Two girls, Audrey and Joan, ran to me at once. "Anything wrong, can we help?" They were really kind to break their rhythm to help me. Their concern and a straightened out sock made me forget about the problem. Or perhaps a few more arose, but I declined the offer of a ride in the sweeping-up bus. 'British Airways Take Better Care of You.' The driver went at a crawling pace, behind me for a bit, teasingly, and I was surprised to see how cheerful, fit and well the runners who'd given up were looking as they waved from the comfort of the bus. Perhaps they'd have looked different standing up.

As we came to a network of roads and crossings, with railings to keep people on the pavements, a voice boomed over loudspeakers: "You are now running at your own risk. Keep to the pavements". And I was on the wrong side of the railings. We came to a long stretch, thickly lined with people, and strangely (but luckily for me) no traffic at all. Then on to Tower Bridge.

This is what makes the London marathon so wonderful to run. There's so much to see, before, during and after the Thames, so much history to divert one's mind from aches and pains, it's like running through the pages of a child's story book.

A TV interviewer was running beside me said, "I'm going to interview you as we go under the second arch. You're better than last time". Yes, Tower Bridge was a cold and deserted place then. Now, it was thick with people; I almost expected to hear the splashes of cartoon figures toppling off into the river below. "This is the most wonderful occasion in my whole life", I blurted out to the interviewer, thinking "Well it comes after having babies". On, past the halfway mark and down crowded Manchester Road. There were more people sensibly going about their business than runners, now.

Above and below my knees, I was perfectly OK and could have gone on and on, but oh, those creaky knees. Having sustained retinal damage, my eye specialist had advised me to stop lifting bags of sugar with my ankles, as the strain could cause further damage. Since I've stopped, my marathon times have been slower, 6.42 and 6.04, which leads me to think there is something in the weights idea.

As a substitute, I sit on the floor and push my knees down hard against the resistance of a rolled-up towel. If I've to sit for any length of time, watching TV, travelling by train, or waiting at the doctor's surgery, I straighten out my legs at right angles to my back, push the knees down hard and hold for five, then release for three.

"You'll run marathons faster now that you've done it before", a friend said to me. But running skills don't work out that way. You've got to work at fitness to maintain it. Witness my creaky knees!

Further along the route, I caught up on a tall man in an orange shirt and we ran together. As we passed groups on flats' balconies, there were shouts "Madge, hello there." and "We've been waiting for you, Madge, now we can go home and get dinner". My companion turned to give me a good look, "You must be a celebrity, Mel Borders is the name. Give me a ring when you come to San Francisco, I've a store there. The running's great. I'm 56 and we've a man of 83 in our club". Mel was hobbling a bit now "It's a war injury". But he still finished ahead of me.

Suddenly a lady dashed out of a car and ran towards me. It was Erika Tedder, my running companion in New York. We linked arms and shuffle-walked along together chatting like a coffee-morning party. Her arm in a sling, with tennis elbow, and one of her three children lost in the crowds in central London, yet she came out to meet me on the Isle of Dogs, and I loved her for it.

The pavements stretched out longer now, and I was thinking of Mike and Ozzie who rushed out to run the last miles to the stadium in Bermuda with me, when suddenly, there were two blazered youths beside me, Mark and Fizz. "We've watched you so often on the video of last year's marathon. May we run with you?" Discussing school, running and sport, I enjoyed their company for a mile or two.

After the '81 London Marathon, I'd written a letter "To, any newspaper, Isle of Dogs. A great big thank you to the kind people of the Isle of Dogs who came out with pots of tea, bottles of milk and jugs of water to refresh the runners when drinks' stations had packed up. And a special thank you to the ladies who danced and sang 'Knees up Mother Brown', specially for me". I was plodding along, alone at that time.

Suddenly, I turned a corner and there were the ladies. They had a huge card of red roses, signed with love and kisses by fifteen of them. They all hugged and kissed me, pressing sweets into my hands, and we linked arms and danced along, singing. Capers like that don't exactly do wonders for your finishing time, but what's a 'personal best' compared to moments like that.

Tower Bridge came along soon after that, and an Aberdonian was waiting for me. "I'm going to pace you to the finishing line", he announced. "Delighted", I answered, "as long as you don't expect me to chat. I need all my breath to keep going". When we came to the Blackwater Underpass, traffic was running and we had to climb stairs to get on to the walkway right by the Thames. Those stairs were agony, but my friend from Aberdeen was literally a tower of strength. I don't think I should have allowed him to take my arm for he wasn't a marathoner, but should or shouldn't, I hadn't the strength to explain, and we just got on with the business of getting to Westminster Bridge.

Embankment traffic was very heavy now, and we looked for the best part to cross to go up Northumberland Street. Just then, Bob Iles, bemedalled (for he'd finished the marathon) came back to look for me. He could take my arm without infringing AAA rules, and when the TV cameras caught us, crossing Trafalgar Square to the Mall (Bob carrying his yellow plastic marathon issue bag with his running gear) we looked like any couple out doing some weekend shopping. Every stop after 15 miles was harder to recover from, and crossing London's streets was a wearisome business. My pace certainly slowed down. I'd been dreading the long triangle of the Embankment, down the Mall and Birdcage Walk, but in reality, it was a hilarious romp, so many people relaxing in the park, rushed forwards for photographs and autographs.

The magic moment was drawing near. Bob had been running behind me, but now, leaving Birdcage Walk, we had a straight run through to Westminster Bridge, and propelling me into the middle of the road, we took our stance in a long queue of traffic and were wafted over on to the bridge.

Suddenly, my arms were outstretched. "You looked as if you'd found the end of the rainbow", said a friend. I had. Chris Brasher was on the finishing line holding out his arms to envelop me with hugs and kisses. That was heaven, to finish with this most wonderful welcome of all. Tony Gubba was there too, and TV cameras, but I was oblivious

At the end of the Second London Marathon

to that. I was just chatting to friends, Chris and Tony. Then our eyes met, and we kissed again, "Oh Chris", I sighed with happiness. The lion statue on the bridge mutely impassive. Through the funnel to where John Disley was ready to slip my medal over my head. A queue of people were waiting for photographs. My friend Edna Sorrell captured the ecstasy and the sweat. I sat down in the sunshine to autograph a pile of papers. I'd finished in 6 hours 14 minutes 58 seconds.

Sylvia Disley extended a welcome arm, "I'm taking you to the West Nally tent for some champagne." I knew I ought to be at the Muscular Dystrophy Group Reception, but I was too late for that. And to go and check if anyone was still waiting there, meant a long walk. So, feeling guilty, that I ought to have hobbled along and checked, I refreshed myself with the champagne, and was driven back to the Cavendish by Sylvia, with her lovely daughters.

To David Hunn in the *Observer*, I was 'the Divine Madge Sharples', to Nancy Banks-Smith in the *Guardian*, 'Mad Madge'.

Harry Carpenter (team captain) wrote to me:

123, Andover Road,
Winchester,
Hants. SO23 7EQ

Dear Madge,

You did it! Congratulations on completing what must have been a gruelling 26.2 miles on a very warm May morning, and many thanks for your support of our MIRRORTHON (Muscular Dystrophy) TEAM.

By supporting the Team you have helped us to attract runners, publicity and funds to the Group and have therefore played an invaluable role in the success of this venture.

The Group's vital research work has benefited substantially from the efforts of you and the TEAM and already over £50,000 has been received at Nattrass House. That is enough to provide the entire financial needs of two typical research projects over a year and will give a real stimulus to the doctors and scientists involved to accelerate their efforts.

I hope that you enjoyed the day as much as I did. In the Recovery Reception I experienced some of the extraordinary team spirit and of the wonderful sense of personal achievement which must have pulled you through. It was a sporting occasion that I shall never forget.

Many thanks, once again, for all that you have done, and my best wishes.

Yours sincerely,

By kind permission of Harry Carpenter.

"An incredibly wonderful day", I wrote in the 'Madge Sharples Column' in *Running*, "Last year, I could have hugged the whole world. This year, I think I did."

And the way to my new extended life lay open.

Another race hath been, and other palms are won.
Thanks to the human heart by which we live.
Thanks to the tenderness, its joys, and fears.
To me the meanest flower that blows can give
Thoughts that do often lie too deep for tears.

Wordsworth, Ode. *Intimations of Immortality*, XI